MW00830275

Rediscovering Your Self Worth

Embracing Self-Love to Open Doors to an
Amazing Life

Sabrina Crumpton

Copyright © 2024 By Sabrina Crumpton

All rights reserved. No part of this book may be used or reproduced by any means, graphic, electronic, or mechanical, including photocopying, recording, taping, or by any information storage retrieval system, without the written permission of the publisher except in the case of brief quotations embodied in critical articles and reviews.

"A Journey to Healing, Empowerment, and Transforming Your Life from Within."

A Transformative Guide to:

- Reclaiming your self-worth
- Building radical self-love
- Overcoming self-doubt
- Crafting a life rooted in your values
- Attracting meaningful relationships

"Your worth isn't something you earn; it's something you reclaim. This is your journey to rediscover the amazing person you've always been."

— Sabrina

Contents

Intro: Rediscovering Your Worth

"Your worth isn't something you earn; it's something you reclaim. This is your journey to rediscover the amazing person you've always been."

- Sabrina

Sabrina's Story: From Heartbreak to Healing

2019 was the year everything changed for me. What started as whispers of discomfort in my marriage quickly spiraled into a storm I never anticipated. My world cracked open the night I discovered the truth, the betrayal, the lies, the secrets. But what hurt the most wasn't what my husband had done. It was the realization that, somewhere along the way, I had lost myself.

I had spent so much of my life trying to be enough for everyone else, enough for my partner, enough for my career, enough for the expectations placed on me. I didn't even know what being *enough* for myself felt like anymore. That moment, standing in the shattered pieces of my marriage, was my rock bottom. But it was also my turning point.

Healing didn't happen overnight. It wasn't easy or linear. But step by step, I began to peel back the layers of self-doubt, guilt, and pain. I confronted the stories I had been telling myself about who I was and what I deserved. I learned to love myself, not the perfect, polished version I thought the world wanted, but the messy, authentic, resilient woman I truly was.

Through this process, I discovered the transformative power of self-worth. It didn't just save me, it became the foundation for a life I could truly thrive in. And that's why I'm here, sharing this with you.

Why Rediscovering Your Worth Is Life-Changing

Have you ever felt like you were running on empty, trying to give and give while barely holding on yourself? Or maybe you've looked in the mirror and questioned whether you were truly deserving of love, success, or even happiness. If you've ever felt this way, let me tell you something important: *You are not alone.*

In fact, studies show that nearly 80% of women struggle with feelings of inadequacy at some point in their lives. That's four out of five of us who doubt our abilities, our beauty, or our worth. But here's the truth: those doubts aren't the final word on your life. They're just stories you've learned along the way, and stories can be rewritten.

Rediscovering your worth is about more than feeling good about yourself. It's about reclaiming your life. It's about breaking free from the patterns that have kept you stuck, setting boundaries that honor your value, and creating a life that reflects the amazing person you are.

This isn't just a feel-good message, it's a call to action.

What to Expect from This Book: A Journey of Growth and Healing

This book is your roadmap to rediscovering your worth. It's filled with the same lessons, tools, and strategies I used to rebuild my life from the ground up. But it's also infused with the wisdom of the women I've worked with, women who, like you, were ready to stop settling for less and start living fully.

Through these pages, you'll:

- Identify the roots of self-doubt and learn how to release its grip.
- Redefine what "enough" means on your own terms.
- Practice radical self-compassion and learn to forgive yourself.
- Envision a life built on self-worth and take actionable steps to create it.
- Cultivate daily habits that reinforce your value and resilience.

Each chapter is designed to inspire and empower you with stories, practical tools, and exercises that will help you transform your mindset and your life.

This book isn't just about reading, it's about doing. Throughout these chapters, you'll find exercises and worksheets designed to help you apply what you're learning in real time. These aren't just theoretical ideas; they're actionable steps that will move you closer to the life you deserve.

You'll also read stories from women who have walked this path before you, real people who faced their fears, embraced their worth, and transformed their lives. Their journeys will remind you that change is possible and that you don't have to do this alone.

If you're holding this book, I believe you're ready for something more. Maybe you've been waiting for permission to prioritize yourself. Maybe you've been searching for a way out of the patterns that no longer serve you. Or maybe you're just curious about what life could look like if you truly believed in your worth.

Whatever brought you here, I want you to know this: *This is your moment.*

It's time to stop waiting for the right circumstances, the right partner, or the right opportunity to show up. Everything you need to create an amazing life is already inside you. All you have to do is begin.

Are you ready? But before we take this journey together, some foundational mindset pillars you must hold dear.

- Your worth isn't something to prove or earn, it's something to rediscover.
- Self-doubt is learned and can be unlearned.
- This book will guide you through practical steps, inspiring stories, and powerful exercises to transform your mindset and your life.
- The journey starts now, and you are more than capable of taking the first step.

1: The Weight of Self-Doubt

Recognizing and Releasing Internal Barriers
The Invisible Anchor

Self-doubt doesn't announce itself loudly or dramatically. It's not the storm that knocks you off course; it's the quiet, invisible anchor that keeps you from setting sail in the first place. It whispers to you in moments of vulnerability, planting seeds of hesitation and fear. Over time, it becomes so familiar, you may not even realize it's there.

For years, I carried this anchor. I didn't call it self-doubt back then, I called it being realistic, cautious, or "humble." It whispered to me that I wasn't good enough to ask for what I needed in my marriage, that my dreams were too big or impractical, and that if something in my life wasn't working, it must be my fault.

But here's the thing about self-doubt: it thrives on lies. And those lies can rob you of your potential, your joy, and your ability to truly see yourself.

A Personal Moment: Sabrina's Story

I remember the night I discovered my husband's betrayal. I was standing in my living room, holding his phone, the evidence of his infidelity glaring back at me. My heart broke into a million pieces, not just because of what he had done, but because of the thoughts that immediately filled my mind:

- "What did I do wrong?"

- "Why wasn't I enough?"
- "Maybe if I had been better, this wouldn't have happened."

That night, I realized just how deeply self-doubt had woven itself into my life. Even in a moment where the blame was not mine to carry, I instinctively turned inward, questioning my own worth.

It was a painful wake-up call, but also a powerful one. I began to see the stories I'd been telling myself for what they were: lies. Lies that had taken root in my heart over the years, whispering that I wasn't deserving of love, respect, or success.

That moment marked the beginning of my journey to unlearn those lies and rediscover the truth: *I was always enough. I just didn't believe it yet.*

Self-doubt is subtle but powerful. It doesn't crash into your life all at once; it sneaks in, disguising itself as "practicality" or "being realistic." It convinces you that:

- Your dreams are out of reach.
- You're not as capable as others.
- You shouldn't ask for more because you don't deserve it.

It might show up when you hesitate to apply for a promotion or start a project you're passionate about. It's there when you stay in a relationship that drains you because you're afraid no one else will love you. It's even in the way you look at yourself in the mirror, finding flaws instead of strength.

The insidious nature of self-doubt is what makes it so dangerous. It doesn't just keep you stuck, it convinces you that staying stuck is the only option.

What This Chapter Will Do for You

If any of this feels familiar, you're not alone. Self-doubt is one of the most universal struggles, but it's also one of the most misunderstood. Many of us think self-doubt is just part of who we are, a personality trait we have to live with. But that's not true. Self-doubt is a learned behavior, and what is learned can be unlearned.

In this chapter, we'll:

- Dive deep into the roots of self-doubt, exploring where it comes from and why it's so persistent.

- Identify how self-doubt shows up in your life, from procrastination to people-pleasing.

- Examine the real cost of self-doubt, the opportunities missed, the relationships harmed, and the emotional toll it takes.

- Begin building the tools you need to challenge and overcome it.

My hope is that as you move through this chapter, you'll start to recognize self-doubt for what it truly is: not a reflection of your worth, but a barrier you have the power to dismantle.

This isn't just about feeling better or more confident. It's about reclaiming your life. Each time you challenge the lies of self-doubt, you take a step toward the person you were always meant to be. So, let this be your starting point.

Take a deep breath, and let's begin the journey together. You are so much more than the stories self-doubt has told you, and by the end of this chapter, you'll begin to see that for yourself.

Understanding the Psychology and Origin of Self-Doubt

Self-doubt is like an invisible shadow, following you everywhere. It's the voice that questions your worth, your abilities, and even your right to dream. It doesn't yell or scream; it whispers, quietly enough that you might not even realize it's there. But its words are powerful:

- "You're not smart enough to do this."
- "Who are you to think you deserve more?"
- "What if you fail? Everyone will see."

You're not alone if you've heard these whispers before. For so many of us, self-doubt feels like a constant companion, an unwelcome guest that lingers in our minds and hearts. If you've ever felt like you weren't enough or questioned your right to take up space, I want you to know something: *there's nothing wrong with you.*

Self-doubt isn't your truth. It's not who you are, it's something you've learned. And just as it was learned, it can be unlearned.

It's important to understand that self-doubt doesn't appear out of nowhere. It has roots, often buried deep in our experiences, our environments, and the messages we've absorbed over the years. The reasons it shows up might be different for each of us, but the feelings it creates are universal.

1. Early Experiences

Many of us carry the weight of messages we heard in childhood. Maybe someone told you that you weren't smart enough, creative enough, or strong enough. Maybe you grew up in an environment where love felt conditional, based on your achievements, appearance, or ability to make others happy.

Those words, those moments, stay with us. They become the stories we tell ourselves, even when they no longer serve us.

2. Past Failures and Rejections

Failure can be one of life's greatest teachers, but it can also leave scars. Maybe you tried something once and it didn't work out. You told yourself, *"I'll never put myself in that position again."* Over time, fear of failure builds walls around you, keeping you from trying, risking, or dreaming.

3. Comparison Culture

We live in a world where we're constantly shown the best parts of other people's lives. On social media, we see the promotions, the vacations, the picture-perfect relationships. What we don't see are the struggles behind the scenes. And yet, it's so easy to look at those curated images and think, *"Why am I so far behind?"*

4. Internalized Criticism

Sometimes the harshest critic lives inside of us. Maybe someone in your life, a parent, a teacher, a partner, planted those seeds of doubt with their words or actions. Over time, their voice became your voice, replaying those same messages over and over.

5. Trauma and Betrayal

Experiences of betrayal, abandonment, or heartbreak can deeply shake your sense of worth. When someone you trusted hurts you, it's easy to turn the blame inward: *"If I had been better, maybe this wouldn't have happened."*

How Self-Doubt Protects and Limits You

If you see yourself in any of these stories, take a deep breath. There's nothing wrong with you for feeling this way. Self-doubt doesn't mean you're weak or flawed, it means you're human. It means you've lived, loved, and cared deeply enough to be shaped by your experiences.

Self-doubt often disguises itself as self-protection. It convinces you that staying small is safer than taking risks, that not trying is better than failing, and that settling for less is easier than facing rejection.

But here's the thing: while self-doubt might shield you from temporary discomfort, it also keeps you from experiencing growth, joy, and fulfillment.

- **The Comfort Zone Trap:**
  - Self-doubt tells you, *"If I don't try, I can't fail."* But the reality is, staying stuck is its own form of failure.
- **Self-Sabotage:**
  - It might make you procrastinate on opportunities you're excited about because deep down, you fear success as much as failure.

Interactive Reflection: Where Does Your Self-Doubt Come From?

Take a moment to reflect on your own experiences.

- *Can you remember a time when someone's words or actions planted a seed of doubt in your mind?*

- *Are there specific situations or triggers where self-doubt shows up most often?*

Write down three moments or patterns where you've noticed self-doubt in your life.

As you think about these patterns, I want you to do something important: be kind to yourself. It's easy to feel frustrated or ashamed when we see how self-doubt has shaped our lives. But remember, self-doubt isn't your fault. It's a response to the experiences you've had, it's your mind's way of trying to keep you safe.

The fact that you're reading this, that you're willing to face those doubts, shows incredible courage.

How Self-Doubt Shapes Our Lives

Self-doubt doesn't always look the way you might expect. It doesn't show up with flashing lights, boldly announcing, *"I'm here to hold you back!"* Instead, it's subtle, weaving itself into your thoughts, decisions, and behaviors in ways that can be hard to notice. It's not until you take a step back that you realize just how much of your life it's influenced.

The truth is, self-doubt can show up in any area of your life, your career, your relationships, your goals, and it often wears disguises that make it hard to identify.

Common Manifestations of Self-Doubt

1. Procrastination

Procrastination is one of self-doubt's favorite tricks. You tell yourself you're "waiting for the right time, " or that you're "not ready yet, " but beneath those excuses is often a fear of not being good enough.

- *Example:* You've been wanting to start a side hustle for months, but every time you sit down to plan, you find a reason to delay. "I just need to take one more course, " you tell yourself, even though you already have all the knowledge you need to begin.

Procrastination isn't laziness, it's often fear in disguise. It's the fear of starting and failing, or even starting and succeeding, because success might bring new expectations.

2. Overthinking

Have you ever spent hours agonizing over a decision, replaying every possible outcome in your head? That's self-doubt at work, convincing you that there's a "perfect" choice and that making the wrong one will be catastrophic.

- *Example:* You're debating whether to apply for a promotion at work. You've listed out every possible pro and con, asked for advice from friends, and stayed up late researching the role. But still, you hesitate. "What if I'm not qualified? What if I mess up? What if they laugh at me for even trying?"

Overthinking creates a cycle of paralysis. The more you analyze, the harder it feels to take action, and the harder it feels to take action, the more you doubt yourself.

3. Settling for Less

Self-doubt has a way of convincing you that you don't deserve more. It whispers, *"Who do you think you are to want better?"* Whether it's in your career, your relationships, or your dreams, self-doubt pushes you to accept what's in front of you, even if it's far from what you truly want.

- *Example*: You're in a relationship that doesn't fulfill you, but the thought of leaving feels overwhelming. What if you never find someone else? What if this is as good as it gets?

Settling for less isn't about laziness or lack of ambition, it's about fear. It's the fear of stepping into the unknown, of risking rejection, or of finding out that the life you want isn't as easy to achieve as you hoped.

4. Avoidance

Avoidance is another way self-doubt keeps you stuck. Instead of facing challenges head-on, you steer clear of situations that might trigger those feelings of inadequacy.

- *Example*: You've always wanted to write a book, but every time you sit down to start, you feel overwhelmed. So, you avoid it altogether, telling yourself, "I'll try when I have more time."

Avoidance feels safe at the moment, but it comes with a cost. Every time you avoid something important to you, you reinforce the belief that you can't handle it.

5. Downplaying Achievements

Even when you accomplish something great, self-doubt can show up as the inability to own your success. Instead of celebrating, you dismiss your achievements, telling yourself it was luck or that it "wasn't a big deal."

- *Example*: A client I once worked with landed a dream job, but when I congratulated her, she shrugged and said, "They must have just been desperate to fill the position." She couldn't see that her hard work and qualifications were what earned her that role.

When you downplay your achievements, you rob yourself of the confidence boost that comes from acknowledging your success.

Why Self-Doubt Shows Up in These Ways

Self-doubt doesn't manifest randomly, it shows up where it hurts the most. It targets the areas of your life where you feel the most vulnerable, whether that's your career, your relationships, or your sense of purpose.

It also thrives in silence. The less you acknowledge or challenge it, the more power it gains. That's why it's so important to recognize these patterns for what they are, not reflections of your worth, but symptoms of a deeper belief that you're not enough.

Interactive Reflection: Spotting Self-Doubt in Your Life

Take a moment to reflect on your own life. Where does self-doubt show up the most for you?

- *Do you find yourself procrastinating on certain goals?*
- *Are you overthinking decisions or avoiding opportunities?*

- *Do you settle for less in your relationships or career?*

Write down three areas where you've noticed self-doubt showing up. Be honest with yourself, this isn't about judgment, it's about awareness.

Stories of Self-Doubt in Action

Sabrina's Story

In my marriage, self-doubt kept me stuck for far longer than I should have stayed. I convinced myself that if I just tried harder, if I were better, things would change. When I discovered my husband's betrayal, my first thought wasn't anger, it was shame.

I wondered, *"What did I do wrong? Wasn't I good enough?"*

Looking back, I can see how deeply self-doubt had rooted itself in my life. I had internalized the belief that I wasn't deserving of respect or love, and that belief kept me from seeing the truth: I didn't need to be better. I was always enough.

Sarah's Story

Sarah was a talented artist who dreamed of showcasing her work in galleries, but self-doubt kept her art hidden. She told herself, *"No one will care about my work. What if they think it's terrible?"*

When we began working together, Sarah started tracking her thoughts and noticing how often self-doubt stopped her from taking action. Through exercises and reframing, she began to see her art as valuable, not because of how others might perceive it, but because it was an expression of her soul.

Eventually, Sarah took the leap and shared her work at a local art show. The response was overwhelmingly positive, but more importantly, she realized she didn't need external validation to feel proud of her creativity.

Self-doubt shows up in so many ways, but it doesn't have to control your life. By recognizing these patterns, you're already taking the first step toward breaking free. In the next section, we'll explore the true cost of self-doubt, the opportunities missed, the emotional toll, and the relationships impacted.

Remember: you are not your self-doubt. You are stronger, braver, and more capable than the lies it tells you. Let's continue this journey together.

The Cost of Self-Doubt

Self-doubt doesn't just linger quietly in the background; it actively chips away at your life, one missed opportunity, one compromised decision, one strained relationship at a time. It's not just a feeling, it's a thief, stealing your confidence, your joy, and your ability to live fully.

But here's the thing: self-doubt often disguises its true cost. It whispers, *"I'm protecting you from failure,"* or *"It's better to play it safe."* What it doesn't tell you is what it's taking from you in the process.

In this section, we'll explore the emotional, professional, and personal toll of self-doubt and what it truly costs you when you let it run unchecked.

1. Missed Opportunities

Every time self-doubt convinces you to say no to something you want, you miss out on a chance to grow, learn, or thrive. It creates a barrier between you and the opportunities waiting for you, leaving you stuck in a cycle of hesitation.

Career

In your career, self-doubt might show up as hesitation to apply for a promotion, start a business, or pursue a passion project. It whispers, *"What if you're not good enough?"* or *"What if you fail?"*

- *Example*: A client of mine once passed on a leadership role because she didn't think she was "ready." The person who got the position had less experience than her, but they believed in themselves enough to try.

Personal Goals

Self-doubt also keeps you from pursuing personal dreams. Maybe you've always wanted to write a book, start a nonprofit, or take a solo trip, but every time you think about it, that voice tells you, *"You don't have what it takes."*

Reflection

Take a moment to think about an opportunity you've let pass you by because of self-doubt. What might have been different if you had taken the leap?

2. Emotional Toll

Self-doubt isn't just about what you don't do, it's also about how it makes you feel. Over time, living with constant doubt takes a toll on your mental and emotional well-being.

Anxiety and Overthinking

Self-doubt feeds anxiety by making you over analyze every decision and second-guess your abilities. It creates a constant loop of "what ifs" that leave you feeling stuck and overwhelmed.

- *Example*: You're invited to speak at an event, but instead of feeling excited, you spiral into questions like, *"What if I mess up?"* or *"What if people think I'm not qualified?"* The opportunity becomes a source of stress instead of growth.

Shame and Low Self-Esteem

At its core, self-doubt often stems from shame, the belief that you're not enough. Over time, it erodes your self-esteem, making it harder to see your strengths or value.

- *Sabrina's Story*: "When I discovered my husband's betrayal, my first instinct wasn't anger, it was shame. I thought, *'What did I do wrong? Why wasn't I enough?'* Looking back, I can see how much self-doubt shaped my reaction. It made me believe the problem was me, even when it wasn't."

3. Strained Relationships

Self-doubt doesn't just affect how you see yourself, it impacts how you show up in your relationships. When you doubt your worth, you're more likely to:

- **Accept Less Than You Deserve**: Staying in toxic relationships or friendships because you don't believe you're worthy of better.

- **Fear Vulnerability**: Holding back in relationships because you're afraid of being rejected or misunderstood.

- **Overcompensate**: Trying too hard to prove your worth to others, often at the expense of your own needs.

Example: Staying in a Toxic Relationship

A former client, Maria, stayed in a relationship where her partner constantly belittled her. She told herself, *"I should just be grateful someone wants to be with me."* It wasn't until she began working on her self-worth that she realized she deserved so much more.

Reflection

Think about your relationships. Are there dynamics where self-doubt has caused you to settle, hold back, or overextend yourself?

4. Self-Sabotage

One of the most subtle but damaging costs of self-doubt is self-sabotage. When you don't believe in yourself, you unconsciously create obstacles that prevent you from succeeding.

- **Procrastination**: Delaying projects or goals because you're afraid of failing.

- **Undermining Success**: Downplaying your achievements or avoiding opportunities to grow.

- **Setting Low Expectations**: Choosing paths that feel "safe" instead of pursuing what you truly want.

- *Example*: A writer I once coached had an incredible book idea but kept putting off writing it. "What if no one reads it?" she said. When she finally pushed through her doubts, she not only finished the book but received glowing feedback from readers.

5. The Ripple Effect: A Life Half-Lived

The most profound cost of self-doubt isn't just missed opportunities or strained relationships, it's the life you don't live. When you let self-doubt guide your choices, you end up settling for a version of life that feels smaller than what you're capable of.

Imagine looking back five or ten years from now and realizing that the only thing standing between you and your dreams was a belief that wasn't even true.

Reflection Prompt

Take a moment to write down an area of your life where you've held back because of self-doubt. Then, ask yourself:

- What might be possible if I chose to believe in myself instead?

- What's the first small step I could take to move forward?

Turning Awareness Into Action

The cost of self-doubt is real, but so is the opportunity to change. By recognizing where it shows up and how it impacts your life, you're already taking the first step toward reclaiming your confidence and power.

In the next section, we'll dive into practical tools and strategies to challenge self-doubt and begin rewriting the stories it's told you. Remember, awareness is the foundation of transformation. You've already started the process by reading this far.

Practical Steps to Recognize and Release Self-Doubt

Recognizing self-doubt is the first step in loosening its grip on your life. Once you see it for what it is, a learned pattern, not a reflection of your worth, you can begin to challenge it and replace it with empowering thoughts and actions. In this section, we'll explore actionable strategies to help you break free from self-doubt and step into your full potential.

1. Identify the Voice of Self-Doubt

Self-doubt often feels like a part of who you are, but it's not. It's just a voice, one you've likely absorbed from past experiences or external influences. The key to overcoming it is separating that voice from your true self.

Exercise: The Self-Doubt Journal

For one week, keep a journal of the moments when self-doubt arises. Write down:

- The thought: What is self-doubt telling you?
- The trigger: What situation or person brought this thought up?
- The impact: How did this thought influence your behavior?

Example:

- Thought: "I'll mess up if I speak in this meeting."
- Trigger: Being asked to share an idea at work.
- Impact: I stayed silent even though I had something valuable to say.

By identifying patterns, you'll start to see when and where self-doubt tends to appear, making it easier to challenge.

2. Challenge the Lies of Self-Doubt

Self-doubt thrives on assumptions, not facts. To dismantle it, you need to question its validity.

How to Challenge Self-Doubt

When a self-doubt thought arises, ask yourself:

- *"Is this thought based on fact or fear?"*
- *"What evidence do I have that supports or contradicts this thought?"*
- *"What would I say to a friend if they had this thought?"*

Reframing Exercise

Take one recurring self-doubt belief and reframe it into a positive, empowering statement.

Example:

- Self-Doubt Thought: "I'm not good enough to start my own business."
- Reframe: "I have unique skills and experiences that make me capable of building something great. I can start small and grow over time."

Write down your new affirmations and repeat them daily to replace the old narratives.

3. Focus on Your Strengths

Self-doubt loves to fixate on your perceived weaknesses. To counteract this, shift your focus to your strengths, the qualities and achievements that make you uniquely valuable.

Exercise: Strengths Inventory

- Write down three things you're proud of accomplishing, big or small.

- List five qualities you admire about yourself (e.g., kindness, resilience, creativity).

- Reflect on how these strengths have helped you in challenging situations before.

Example:

- Strength: "I'm resilient, I've overcome difficult times before."

- Reflection: "Even when things felt impossible, I found a way to move forward. I can do that again."

Place this list somewhere you'll see it often as a reminder of your capabilities.

4. Take Small, Intentional Steps

Self-doubt thrives on inaction. The longer you wait to take a step, the more power it gains. But you don't have to leap into the unknown all at once, small, intentional actions can be just as effective in building confidence.

The "One Small Step" Method

- Choose one area where self-doubt has been holding you back.
- Break your goal into the smallest possible step you can take today.
- Celebrate each small win as progress.

Example:

- Goal: Starting a fitness routine.
- Small Step: Putting on workout clothes and stretching for five minutes.
- Celebrate: Acknowledge the effort you made, no matter how small.

Each small step builds momentum and reinforces the belief that you are capable.

5. Visualize Your Success

Visualization is a powerful tool for rewiring your brain and shifting your mindset. When you picture yourself succeeding, you train your mind to believe it's possible.

Exercise: Visualization Practice

- Close your eyes and take a deep breath.
- Picture yourself achieving a goal you've been hesitant to pursue.
  - What does it look like?
  - How do you feel?
  - Who is there to celebrate with you?

- Write down this vision in detail, as if it's already happened.

Example:

"I see myself confidently presenting my ideas at work. My colleagues are engaged and supportive. I feel proud of my contribution, knowing I've stepped out of my comfort zone."

Revisit this visualization daily to reinforce your belief in your ability to succeed.

6. Practice Daily Affirmations

Affirmations are short, positive statements that help rewire your thought patterns. When repeated consistently, they can replace self-doubt with self-belief.

How to Use Affirmations

- Choose affirmations that resonate with you (e.g., "I am capable, " "I deserve success").

- Write them on sticky notes and place them where you'll see them often (e.g., your mirror or desk).

- Repeat them aloud each morning or whenever self-doubt arises.

Examples:

- "I am enough just as I am."

- "Every day, I grow stronger and more confident."

- "I am capable of handling whatever comes my way."

7. Build a Support System

Self-doubt can feel isolating, but you don't have to face it alone. Surrounding yourself with supportive people who believe in you can make a world of difference.

How to Build Your Circle of Support

- Seek Encouragers: Share your goals with friends or mentors who lift you up.

- Find a Community: Join groups or communities that align with your interests and values.

- Work with a Coach: Sometimes, professional guidance can help you break through self-doubt faster.

Client Story:

One of my clients, Maria, felt stuck in her career because of self-doubt. When she began working with me, we focused on creating a plan for her next steps and building her confidence. With support and accountability, she applied for, and got, a promotion she had hesitated to pursue for years.

8. Reflect and Adjust

Self-doubt isn't something you overcome overnight, it's a process. Regular reflection helps you track your progress and adjust your strategies as needed.

Exercise: Weekly Self-Doubt Check-In

- What progress did I make this week?
- Where did self-doubt show up?

- How did I respond to it?

- What can I do differently next week?

By regularly reflecting on your journey, you'll gain insight into your patterns and continue building resilience.

Turning Tools Into Transformation

The strategies in this section aren't just exercises, they're tools for transformation. Each time you track a negative thought, reframe it, or take a small step forward, you're actively rewriting the story self-doubt has told you.

Remember, self-doubt is not your truth, it's just a voice. And with practice, you can turn the volume down on that voice and turn up the belief in yourself.

You've already taken the first step by reading this chapter. Now, it's time to put these tools into action and begin reclaiming your confidence and power.

Lifting the Anchor

Self-doubt may feel like an unshakable part of who you are, but it's not your truth. It's a story, a story shaped by your past experiences, fears, and the expectations of others. The beauty of stories, though, is that they can be rewritten. You are the author of your life, and you hold the power to tell a new story, one where self-doubt is no longer the protagonist.

As we've explored in this chapter, self-doubt manifests in many ways: procrastination, overthinking, settling for less, and even self-sabotage. But it doesn't have to define you. By recognizing its patterns, challenging its lies, and taking small, intentional steps forward, you can begin to reclaim your confidence and step into the life you deserve.

Think of Maria, who doubted her ability to ask for more in her career and relationships. By tracking her self-doubt and reframing her beliefs, she found the courage to take steps that changed her life, landing her a job she once thought was out of reach and reigniting her self-worth.

Or Sarah, the artist who kept her work hidden out of fear that it wasn't "good enough." Through visualization and small acts of bravery, she shared her art with the world and discovered the joy of being seen and appreciated.

These women aren't special in the sense that they had something you don't. Their stories are proof of what's possible when you choose to challenge self-doubt and embrace your potential. Like them, you are capable of transformation.

Now it's your turn. You've already taken the first step by reading this chapter and reflecting on where self-doubt shows up in your life. The next step is action, no matter how small it might feel.

- Start journaling your self-doubt triggers.
- Write down an affirmation and say it to yourself every morning.
- Take one small step toward a goal you've been hesitant to pursue.

Remember, transformation doesn't happen overnight. It happens in the moments when you choose courage over comfort, belief over fear, and action over hesitation.

Imagine this: a year from now, you look back at this moment and see it as the turning point. You've accomplished goals you once thought were out of reach. You've spoken up in meetings, applied for the dream job, or taken the leap into a new relationship. Most importantly, you've built a relationship with yourself that is rooted in trust, compassion, and belief.

This is what's waiting for you on the other side of self-doubt: a life that feels authentic, fulfilling, and yours.

As one of my clients once said:

"Sabrina showed me that self-doubt isn't a life sentence, it's a challenge. And with her guidance, I realized I had the tools to meet that challenge all along."

You, too, have those tools. You've always had them. The exercises, stories, and strategies in this chapter are here to help you uncover and use them. With each step, you'll build confidence and momentum, proving to yourself that you are capable of more than you ever imagined.

So take a deep breath, hold onto the truth of your worth, and take that first step. You don't have to see the whole path right now, you just need to start walking. Your journey to rediscovering your confidence and rewriting the story of self-doubt begins today.

Let's move forward together.

2: Redefining "Enough" – Reclaiming Your Self-Worth

Breaking Free from the Chase and Embracing Your Inherent Value

The Illusion of "Enough"

How many times have you told yourself, *"If I just achieve this one thing, then I'll finally feel like I'm enough?"* Maybe it's landing the perfect job, reaching a milestone in your relationship, or losing that last five pounds. You might even get there, achieve the goal, tick the box, celebrate for a moment, but then, almost inevitably, the feeling fades. The goalpost moves. You find yourself back on the treadmill, chasing the elusive idea of "enough" all over again.

It's exhausting, isn't it? This endless pursuit, this constant striving for a feeling of worthiness that seems just out of reach. The world around us tells us we'll find it in the next accomplishment, the next relationship, or the next approval from someone we care about. But no matter how much we do or how much we achieve, that feeling of "not enough" lingers, whispering that we still have more to prove.

Sabrina's Story: The Weight of Never Feeling Enough

For years, I lived this way. I thought if I could just be the perfect partner, the perfect caregiver, the perfect version of myself, then maybe I'd feel worthy. In my marriage, I poured every ounce of myself into trying to make things work. I told myself it was my job to keep the peace, to shoulder the blame, to do whatever it took to be "good enough."

But the harder I tried, the more drained and disconnected I felt. When the betrayal finally came, when I discovered my husband's infidelity, it shattered me. Not just because of what he did, but because of what it made me believe about myself.

I remember thinking, *"What did I do wrong? Why wasn't I enough?"* I couldn't see, in that moment, that my worth had nothing to do with his actions. I had spent so much of my life tying my sense of value to what I could do for others that I had forgotten how to value myself simply for being.

Looking back now, I see that the problem wasn't that I wasn't enough, it was that I didn't believe I was.

The Cultural and Societal Illusions of "Enough"

The truth is, I'm not alone in feeling this way, and neither are you. So many of us are conditioned to believe that our worth is something we have to earn. Society feeds us the illusion that we'll finally be enough when we:

- Look a certain way.
- Achieve a certain level of success.
- Meet someone else's expectations of who we should be.

Social media only amplifies these messages, bombarding us with highlight reels of other people's lives. We see the perfect vacations, the perfect families, the perfect careers, and we start to wonder: *"Why can't I have that? What's wrong with me?"*

For women especially, the pressure is relentless. We're told that our value lies in our ability to be selfless, to look beautiful, to work hard without complaining, and to always put others first. We're taught that being "enough" means being everything to everyone, an impossible standard that leaves us feeling inadequate no matter how much we do.

This constant striving takes a heavy toll. It leaves us feeling exhausted, anxious, and disconnected from ourselves. When we tie our worth to external achievements or the approval of others, we set ourselves up for a never-ending cycle of comparison and shame.

- We compare our behind-the-scenes struggles to other people's curated highlights.
- We beat ourselves up for not meeting impossible standards.
- We feel anxious about the future, wondering if we'll ever measure up.

Over time, this chase for "enough" doesn't just impact our self-esteem, it spills into every area of our lives. It affects how we show up in relationships, how we pursue our goals, and how we see ourselves in the mirror every morning.

But here's the truth: *You are already enough.* Not because of what you've achieved or how you look or what others think of you, but because of who you are.

Your worth isn't something you have to chase, it's something you were born with. It's inherent, unchanging, and completely independent of external validation. The journey isn't about becoming enough, it's about remembering that you already are.

When you stop tying your worth to things outside of yourself, you free yourself from the endless chase. You create space to live authentically, to pursue your passions, and to build relationships that nourish rather than deplete you.

Setting the Stage for Transformation

This chapter is about reclaiming your definition of "enough." Together, we'll:

- Examine where your beliefs about worthiness come from and how they've shaped your life.

- Challenge the external expectations and societal pressures that don't align with your truth.

- Create a new, empowering definition of enoughness, one that is rooted in self-acceptance and authenticity.

- Explore practical tools and exercises to help you embrace your worth in daily life.

Let this be the moment where the chase ends. You don't have to prove anything to anyone to be worthy. You don't have to achieve, perform, or perfect your way to enoughness. You already have it within you.

Take a deep breath and let that truth sink in: *You are enough, exactly as you are.*

Now, let's begin the journey of remembering it.

The Lies We Believe About Being "Enough"

Have you ever stopped to wonder why you feel the way you do about yourself? Why the words *"I am enough"* feel so hard to believe? That deep ache of "not enough" isn't something you were born with, it's something you've learned. It's a story you've absorbed, shaped by experiences, expectations, and the world around you.

But here's the truth: *that story isn't yours to carry.* You didn't write it. It was written by voices from your past, societal standards you didn't ask for, and the echoes of hurtful moments that were never about you. The good news? You have the power to rewrite it.

Let's look at where this story of "not enough" might have come from.

The Roots of "Not Enough"

1. The Voices from Your Past

For many of us, the seeds of self-doubt were planted in childhood. They came from the people we trusted the most, our parents, caregivers, or teachers. Maybe they didn't mean to hurt us. Maybe they thought they were helping. But their words, their actions, or their silences left marks that shaped how we see ourselves.

- Did you have a parent who constantly criticized you, thinking it would motivate you to do better?
- Were you compared to a sibling, a friend, or even an ideal version of yourself?
- Did you feel like you had to earn love by achieving something, good grades, good behavior, or good looks?

Example: One client told me, "I was always the 'responsible' child. My parents never told me they were proud of me unless I was doing something extraordinary. I grew up thinking my worth was tied to my accomplishments."

The lesson you learned wasn't true, but it felt true: *"I'm only worthy when I'm perfect."*

2. The World's Impossible Standards

The world around us is relentless in telling us we're not enough. Social media, movies, advertisements, they all paint pictures of who we're "supposed" to be:

- Perfectly polished, but effortlessly natural.

- Exceptionally successful, but humble and likable.

- Always giving, but never asking for anything in return.

As women, we're told to shrink ourselves, to be everything for everyone while asking for nothing. We're praised for being selfless, but criticized for not doing more. It's a setup for failure because no matter how hard we try, the world's definition of "enough" is always out of reach.

Example: You scroll through Instagram and see someone's picture-perfect family, their curated home, or their dream vacation. For a moment, you forget that it's just a highlight reel. Instead, you think, *"Why doesn't my life look like that?"*

The comparison cuts deep, and the unspoken message is loud: *"You're not doing enough. You're not enough."*

3. The Pain of Past Wounds

Sometimes, it's not the world or our upbringing that shapes our beliefs, it's the moments when life hurts us the most. A betrayal, a rejection, or a failure can leave scars that whisper, *"You weren't enough to keep them. You weren't enough to succeed. You weren't enough to be loved."*

Sabrina's Story:

"When I discovered my husband's betrayal, my first thought wasn't, *'Why did he do this?'* It was, *'What's wrong with me?'* I felt this crushing wave of shame, as if his actions were proof that I wasn't enough. It took me years to see the truth: his choices had nothing to do with my worth."

The pain we carry from these moments isn't our fault, but it often becomes the lens through which we see ourselves.

4. The Trap of Comparison

Comparison is the thief of joy, yet it's something we do every day. We measure our lives against someone else's highlight reel, forgetting that their journey isn't ours to compare.

But here's the truth: someone else's success doesn't diminish yours. Someone else's beauty doesn't make you less beautiful. Someone else's happiness doesn't mean there's no happiness left for you.

Reflection Exercise

Close your eyes and think of someone you've compared yourself to recently.

- What did you admire about them?
- What story did you tell yourself about why they have what you don't?

- Now, reframe that story. Instead of seeing their success as a reason to feel less, view it as evidence of what's possible for you too.

Example: Instead of thinking, *"She's so confident, I'll never be like her,"* say, *"Her confidence is inspiring. I'm capable of growing into my own."*

The Cost of These Stories

When you live by these learned stories, when you let the voices from your past, the world's standards, or painful experiences define your worth, you lose something precious: your connection to yourself.

- You make decisions based on fear instead of desire.

- You shrink yourself to fit into molds you were never meant to fit.

- You settle for less because you don't believe you deserve more.

But what if you could stop? What if you could let go of these stories and reclaim your worth, not as something you earn, but as something you've always had?

The Beginning of Something New

This isn't where your story ends. It's where it begins. By identifying where these beliefs about "enough" come from, you've already started the process of breaking free. The next step is rewriting your definition, on your terms.

Imagine a life where you wake up each morning and know, deep in your soul, that you are enough. Not because of what you've achieved, but because of who you are. That life is possible, and it starts with a single choice: to let go of what isn't yours to carry and reclaim what always was.

Let's take that step together in the next section. The next section will guide you in creating your own definition of "enough", one that isn't shaped by societal pressures, past experiences, or anyone else's expectations. This is your opportunity to reclaim your worth and step into a life that feels authentic, fulfilling, and entirely your own.

Remember: You are not the product of the world's definitions. You are more than enough, exactly as you are.

Reconnecting with Your Inherent Value

For so long, the world has tried to define what it means to be "enough." It tells you that your worth is tied to how much you achieve, how you look, or how well you meet others' expectations. But what if I told you that none of those definitions matter? What if being "enough" isn't something you achieve, but something you *remember?*

This section is about reclaiming that truth, redefining "enough" on your terms, rooted in your inherent worth. It's about learning to see yourself not through the lens of external validation, but through the unshakable knowledge that your value has always been within you.

1. The Difference Between Intrinsic and Extrinsic Worth

Let's start by understanding the two types of worth:

- **Extrinsic Worth**: This is the worth society tries to sell you. It's tied to external things, your achievements, your appearance, your relationships, your productivity. The problem with extrinsic worth is that it's fragile. It can be taken away or diminished because it relies on things outside of you.

- **Intrinsic Worth**: This is the worth you're born with. It's unchanging and independent of what you do or how others perceive you. It comes from the simple fact that you exist.

To reclaim your sense of enoughness, you need to shift your focus from extrinsic to intrinsic worth. This means letting go of the idea that you need to *do* or *be* anything to be worthy. You already are.

2. Redefining Enough on Your Terms

Step 1: Identify the Old Definitions

The first step in redefining "enough" is to identify the old definitions you've been living by. These might sound like:

- *"I'm only enough when I'm successful at work."*

- *"I'm only enough when I'm in a relationship."*

- *"I'm only enough when I look a certain way."*

Take a moment to reflect on the messages you've absorbed about what it means to be "enough." Where did they come from? Who or what reinforced them?

Step 2: Let Go of What No Longer Serves You

Once you've identified these old definitions, it's time to let them go. This doesn't mean forgetting your past, it means choosing not to let it define you anymore.

Exercise: Write down the old definitions you want to release. Then, tear up the paper or burn it (safely), symbolizing your decision to let go.

3. Crafting Your New Definition

What Does "Enough" Mean to You?

Take a moment to ask yourself:

- What would it feel like to believe I am enough, just as I am?
- What values or qualities do I want to base my sense of worth on?

Your new definition of "enough" should reflect the truth that your worth is inherent, not earned. It might sound like:

- *"I am enough because I exist, and that is reason enough."*
- *"I am worthy of love and respect, regardless of my accomplishments."*
- *"I am enough as I am, flaws and all."*

Write down your new definition and place it somewhere you'll see it every day. Let it become a mantra you return to whenever self-doubt arises.

4. Embodying Enoughness in Daily Life

Redefining "enough" isn't just about changing your thoughts, it's about changing how you live. Here are some ways to embody your new definition of enoughness:

Set Boundaries That Protect Your Worth

When you believe you're enough, you stop tolerating things that undermine your sense of worth. This might mean:

- Saying no to commitments that drain you.
- Walking away from relationships that don't respect you.

- Prioritizing your needs without guilt.

Exercise: Identify one boundary you need to set to honor your worth. Write down how you'll communicate and enforce it.

Celebrate Who You Are, Not Just What You Do

Start celebrating yourself for simply being, not just for what you accomplish. Take moments throughout the day to appreciate your kindness, your resilience, your sense of humor, qualities that have nothing to do with achievement.

Exercise: Each night, write down one thing you love about yourself that's unrelated to productivity or external validation.

Choose Joy Over Perfection

Let go of the need to have everything figured out. Instead of striving for perfection, focus on what brings you joy.

- Wear the outfit you've been saving for a "special occasion."
- Dance around the house for no reason.
- Start the project you've been avoiding because it's "not the right time."

Joy reminds you that you don't need to earn the right to enjoy your life.

5. A Real-Life Example: Sabrina's Journey

When I began redefining my sense of enoughness, it was messy and uncomfortable. I had spent so many years tying my worth to being a caregiver, a partner, and a peacemaker that I didn't know who I was without those roles.

One day, I sat down and wrote this: *"I am enough because I am a child of God. My worth is not something I have to prove, it's something I have to accept."*

At first, I didn't believe it. But every morning, I read it aloud. Every time self-doubt crept in, I reminded myself of those words. Slowly, they began to feel true.

Reclaiming my worth didn't happen overnight. It was a process of unlearning the lies I had carried and replacing them with the truth of who I am. And if I can do it, so can you.

6. Reflection Exercise: Living Your Truth

Take a moment to write down your answers to these questions:

- What old definitions of "enough" am I ready to let go of?
- What new truths about my worth do I want to embrace?
- How can I remind myself of these truths daily?

Keep your answers somewhere you can revisit them often. They're your roadmap to living as the person you were always meant to be.

You've taken a powerful step by redefining "enough" on your terms. This new definition isn't just an idea, it's a foundation. It's the place you'll return to whenever doubt arises, the anchor that keeps you grounded in your inherent worth.

In the next section, we'll explore practical steps to reinforce this new belief and make it a lasting part of your life. Remember, redefining "enough" isn't about becoming someone new, it's about coming home to yourself.

Practical Steps to Redefine "Enough"

Redefining "enough" isn't just about thinking differently, it's about living differently. It's about shifting from a life dictated by external validation and impossible standards to one anchored in self-acceptance and peace. This transformation doesn't happen overnight, and that's okay. True change comes from consistent, intentional action, small, meaningful steps that, over time, rewrite the story you tell yourself about your worth.

Why does this matter? Because living with the belief that you're "not enough" isn't just exhausting, it's limiting. It holds you back from opportunities, joy, and relationships that could fill your life with purpose and connection. It keeps you stuck in a cycle of proving, pleasing, and striving, when what you truly deserve is to *be*.

These exercises aren't just tasks to check off a list, they're tools for liberation. Each one is designed to help you unlearn the lies you've internalized, reconnect with your inherent worth, and start creating a life that reflects the truth of who you are.

This is your opportunity to step out of the shadows of doubt and into a light that has always been within you. These steps will help you not only believe you are enough but live as though you are, and that's where the real transformation begins.

So take a deep breath. This is your moment. Let's begin.

Step 1: Identify and Release External Expectations

The world is full of expectations, many of which don't align with your truth. These might come from society, family, or even your own inner critic. To redefine "enough, " you must let go of the expectations that no longer serve you.

Exercise: The Expectation Audit

- Write down three expectations you feel pressured to meet.
- Next to each one, ask yourself:
  - *"Who does this expectation come from?"*
  - *"Does this align with my values and truth?"*
  - *"What would happen if I let this go?"*
- For each expectation that doesn't align, write down a new belief that supports your sense of enoughness.

Example:

- Expectation: "I need to be perfect at work to be respected."
- New Belief: "My worth isn't tied to my performance. I can do my best without needing to be perfect."

Step 2: Practice Radical Self-Acceptance

Self-acceptance means embracing yourself fully, your strengths, your flaws, your humanity. It's about understanding that your worth isn't diminished by imperfection.

Exercise: Write Yourself a Love Letter

- Write a letter to yourself as if you were speaking to a dear friend.
- Highlight your qualities that have nothing to do with achievements, like your kindness, resilience, or humor.
- Acknowledge any mistakes or shortcomings with compassion.

Example Opening:

"Dear [Your Name],

I want you to know how proud I am of you, not because of what you've accomplished, but because of who you are. Your kindness shines so brightly, and your ability to keep going, even on hard days, inspires me…"

Keep this letter and read it whenever self-doubt arises.

Step 3: Set Boundaries That Protect Your Worth

Your worth deserves protection, and boundaries are the way you honor it. Boundaries communicate to others, and yourself, that your time, energy, and well-being are valuable.

Exercise: Define and Set a Boundary

- Identify one area of your life where you feel overextended or undervalued.

- Write down a boundary you need to set to protect your worth.

- Plan how you'll communicate this boundary to others.

Example:

- Boundary: "I will no longer answer work emails after 7 PM."

- Communication: "I've decided to set aside evenings for personal time, so I won't be checking emails after 7 PM. Thank you for understanding."

Step 4: Create Affirmations Rooted in Self-Worth

Affirmations are powerful tools for reprogramming your mind. When repeated consistently, they help replace self-doubt with self-belief.

Exercise: Build Your Affirmation Toolkit

- Write down three affirmations that reinforce your new definition of "enough."
- Place them where you'll see them daily, on your mirror, desk, or phone screen.
- Say them aloud each morning and whenever self-doubt arises.

Examples:

- "I am enough just as I am."
- "My worth isn't tied to what I achieve, it's inherent."
- "I deserve love, respect, and joy simply because I exist."

Step 5: Celebrate Progress, Not Perfection

The journey to redefining "enough" is not about perfection, it's about progress. Each small step you take is a victory worth celebrating.

Exercise: The Daily Win Journal

- At the end of each day, write down one thing you're proud of, no matter how small.
- Reflect on how this moment affirms your worth.

Example Entry:

- Win: "I spoke up in a meeting today."
- Reflection: "This reminds me that my voice matters, even when I feel nervous."

Step 6: Visualize Your Worth in Action

Visualization helps you internalize your worth by imagining what your life looks like when you fully embrace it.

Exercise: Guided Visualization

- Close your eyes and take a deep breath.
- Picture yourself living as if you fully believed you were enough.
  - What does your day look like?
  - How do you feel?
  - How do you interact with others?
- Write down your vision in detail, as if it's already true.

Example:

"I wake up feeling calm and confident. I take time for myself without guilt, knowing that I deserve care and rest. At work, I share my ideas without hesitation, trusting that my voice matters. My relationships feel balanced and supportive, and I end each day grateful for the life I've created."

Step 7: Surround Yourself with Support

Your environment plays a huge role in how you see yourself. Surround yourself with people and influences that reinforce your worth, not undermine it.

Action Steps

- Identify one person who uplifts and encourages you, and spend more time with them.
- Seek out communities or groups aligned with your values.
- Limit interactions with people or environments that trigger self-doubt.

Redefining "enough" isn't a one-time decision, it's a daily practice. Some days will feel easier than others, but every step you take brings you closer to the life you deserve.

Commit to one of these steps today. Whether it's writing an affirmation, setting a boundary, or celebrating a small win, know that each action reinforces the truth: *You are enough, just as you are.*

Living as "Enough"

As you've journeyed through this chapter, you've taken the first powerful steps toward reclaiming your worth. You've explored the roots of your beliefs about "enough, " challenged the narratives that no longer serve you, and begun redefining what it means to feel worthy, on your terms. This is no small feat. In fact, it's a transformative act of self-love and courage.

Believing you are enough doesn't mean you won't have hard days or moments of doubt. It doesn't mean you'll never feel the pull of comparison or the pressure to prove yourself. But it does mean you now have the tools to stand firm in the truth of your worth, even when the world tries to tell you otherwise.

The Ripple Effect of Redefining "Enough"

When you live from a place of enoughness, everything changes:

- In your relationships, you stop settling for less than you deserve and start showing up as your authentic self.

- In your career, you stop chasing perfection and embrace the value you bring to the table.

- In your daily life, you find more joy, more peace, and more freedom to be who you truly are.

This shift doesn't just affect you, it impacts everyone around you. When you embrace your worth, you inspire others to do the same. You become a beacon of what's possible: a life lived with confidence, authenticity, and grace.

Transformation begins with action. As you move forward, remember that this journey is ongoing. Start small, stay consistent, and celebrate every step you take. Here's how you can continue building on what you've learned in this chapter:

- Revisit your new definition of "enough" daily. Let it guide your decisions and remind you of your inherent worth.

- Commit to one practice, an affirmation, a boundary, a celebration of progress, that reinforces your belief in yourself.

- Reflect regularly on how far you've come, and be patient with yourself as you continue to grow.

If there's one thing I want you to take away from this chapter, it's this: *You are enough.* Not because of what you've done, not because of who approves of you, but because of who you are.

You've always been enough. The world might have made you forget, but you're here now, remembering. And that is the greatest gift you can give yourself, the gift of knowing, deep in your soul, that you are whole, worthy, and complete, just as you are.

Carry this truth with you. Let it anchor you when doubt creeps in and guide you when life feels uncertain. You are enough today, tomorrow, and every day after that.

So stand tall, speak boldly, and live fully. The world needs the light only you can bring. And trust me, your light is more than enough.

3: Practicing Radical Self-Compassion

"Finding Strength in Grace: The Journey to Embracing Yourself Fully"

Embracing Your Unique Journey

Imagine for a moment that your best friend comes to you, tears in their eyes, overwhelmed by a mistake they've made. They tell you how ashamed they feel, how they're convinced they've failed. What would you say to them? Would you criticize them, point out all the ways they've fallen short, and tell them they should have done better? Of course not. You'd likely reassure them, offer comfort, and remind them of all the ways they are still worthy and capable.

Now, think about how you treat yourself in those moments when *you* feel ashamed or overwhelmed. How often do you respond with the same kindness and understanding you'd offer to someone you love? For many of us, the answer is *rarely*.

Self-compassion is the missing link in so many of our lives. It's the bridge between self-doubt and self-belief, between self-criticism and self-acceptance. And yet, it's often the hardest gift to give ourselves.

The Weight of Self-Criticism

For years, I lived under the weight of self-criticism. After my marriage fell apart, I replayed every moment, scrutinizing my actions and choices. I told myself I should have been more patient, more understanding, more *everything.* I blamed myself for the betrayal I experienced, as if my worthiness had somehow caused it.

That inner critic wasn't just a voice, it was a constant presence, dragging me down when I needed to rise. It told me I was weak, unlovable, and inadequate. And for a long time, I believed it.

But then, something shifted. I realized that no amount of self-criticism was going to change my past or heal my pain. In fact, the more I berated myself, the more stuck I felt. What I needed wasn't judgment, it was grace.

What Is Self-Compassion?

Self-compassion is the practice of treating yourself with the same kindness, care, and understanding you'd offer to someone you love. It's not about excusing mistakes or avoiding accountability, it's about creating a foundation of support that allows you to learn, grow, and heal.

When you practice self-compassion, you acknowledge your struggles without letting them define you. You recognize that being human means being imperfect, and that's okay. Self-compassion doesn't make you weak, it makes you resilient.

Here's the truth: You cannot hate yourself into becoming the person you want to be. Growth doesn't come from harsh self-judgment, it comes from self-compassion.

Research shows that self-compassion enhances:

- **Resilience**: People who practice self-compassion are better able to bounce back from setbacks because they view failure as a part of growth, not a reflection of their worth.

- **Confidence**: Self-compassion helps quiet the inner critic, allowing you to pursue your goals with courage and self-belief.

- **Mental Health**: Studies have found that self-compassion reduces anxiety, depression, and stress while increasing overall well-being.

Self-compassion is not self-indulgence or weakness, it's a powerful act of self-respect.

Why It Matters Now

In a world that constantly tells you to do more, be more, and achieve more, self-compassion is a radical act. It's a declaration that you are already enough, even when you fall short of your expectations.

This chapter is an invitation to embrace self-compassion, not as a fleeting moment of kindness, but as a way of life. Together, we'll explore what self-compassion looks like, why it's essential, and how you can begin to integrate it into your daily routine.

Because here's the truth: The relationship you have with yourself sets the tone for every other relationship in your life. When you learn to offer yourself compassion, you create space for healing, growth, and joy.

So take a deep breath. Let go of the judgment, even if just for a moment. This is your time to start speaking to yourself with the kindness and care you've always deserved. Let's begin.

Why Self-Compassion Is Essential

Self-compassion is often misunderstood. Some people think it's indulgent or a sign of weakness. Others believe it's an excuse to avoid accountability. But nothing could be further from the truth. Self-compassion isn't about lowering your standards or letting yourself off the hook, it's about creating a foundation of understanding and care that allows you to grow, even through life's most challenging moments.

The absence of self-compassion leaves a void filled with harsh self-criticism, perfectionism, and shame. Over time, this void drains your energy, confidence, and ability to move forward. But when you choose to embrace self-compassion, you step into a life where mistakes are learning opportunities, setbacks are temporary, and your worth is no longer tied to your flaws or achievements.

The Cost of Self-Criticism

Think about the voice in your head when you make a mistake. Is it kind? Encouraging? Or is it harsh, replaying the failure over and over like a broken record?

For many of us, self-criticism feels automatic. We tell ourselves it's the only way to improve, to "keep ourselves in line." But in reality, self-criticism does the opposite, it paralyzes us.

- **Emotional Toll**: Self-criticism fuels feelings of inadequacy, anxiety, and depression.
- **Impact on Growth**: When you constantly berate yourself, you become afraid to take risks or try new things, fearing failure will bring more self-judgment.

- **Relationship Damage**: Harsh self-criticism often spills over into relationships, making it harder to connect with others authentically.

If you've ever felt stuck, drained, or defeated, self-criticism may be the culprit.

The Benefits of Self-Compassion

Now, imagine if that critical voice in your head was replaced with one of kindness and understanding. How might your life change?

1. Resilience in the Face of Adversity

Self-compassion doesn't eliminate challenges, it equips you to face them. When you treat yourself with kindness, you're more likely to bounce back from setbacks because you see failure as part of growth, not a reflection of your worth.

Example:

A client once shared that after losing her job, she spent months spiraling into shame and self-blame. It wasn't until she began practicing self-compassion, acknowledging her feelings without judgment and reminding herself of her strengths, that she found the courage to start over. Within weeks, she landed a new role that was a better fit for her skills and passions.

2. Increased Confidence

When you replace self-criticism with self-compassion, you free yourself from the fear of imperfection. This shift builds confidence, allowing you to pursue goals and dreams with courage.

3. Improved Mental Health

Studies have shown that self-compassion reduces anxiety, depression, and stress. It's like a safety net for your mental well-being, catching you when life feels overwhelming.

Research by Dr. Kristin Neff, a leading expert on self-compassion, highlights three core elements of the practice:

- **Self-Kindness**: Treating yourself with care rather than criticism.

- **Common Humanity**: Recognizing that everyone struggles, and you're not alone in your challenges.

- **Mindfulness**: Observing your emotions without judgment or exaggeration.

When these elements come together, they create a powerful tool for emotional resilience and personal growth.

Self-compassion doesn't mean you'll never face difficulties. It doesn't mean you won't experience doubt or make mistakes. What it does mean is that when those moments come, you'll have the strength to meet them with grace instead of shame.

You deserve to be treated with the same kindness and care you offer to others. Imagine what your life could look like if you let go of the harshness and replaced it with understanding. Imagine how much lighter, freer, and more empowered you could feel.

Are you ready to meet yourself with kindness? Let's take the next step together.

The Three Elements of Self-Compassion

Self-compassion is like a three-legged stool, each element provides vital support, and together, they create a stable foundation for self-acceptance and growth. According to Dr. Kristin Neff, a leading researcher in self-compassion, these three elements are **self-kindness**, **common humanity**, and **mindfulness**. Let's explore each one in depth.

1. Self-Kindness: Replacing Criticism with Care

Self-kindness is the act of treating yourself with the same understanding and care you would offer a loved one. It's about recognizing that you deserve gentleness, even in moments of failure or pain.

What It Looks Like

- Instead of saying, *"I can't believe I messed up again, "* you say, *"It's okay to make mistakes. I'm learning."*

- Instead of pushing yourself to exhaustion, you give yourself permission to rest and recharge.

Why It Matters

Harsh self-criticism often leads to shame and paralysis, while self-kindness creates a safe space for growth and resilience. When you show yourself kindness, you build trust in your ability to navigate challenges without fear of judgment.

Exercise: Speak to Yourself Like a Friend

The next time you catch yourself being self-critical, pause and ask, *"What would I say to a friend in this situation?"* Write down that response and say it to yourself aloud.

Example:

- Self-Criticism: *"I'll never be good enough to succeed."*
- Self-Kindness: *"This is hard right now, but I'm doing my best, and that's enough."*

2. Common Humanity: You Are Not Alone

When you're struggling, it's easy to feel isolated, as though you're the only one who's ever faced this challenge. Common humanity is the reminder that struggle is part of being human, and you are not alone.

What It Looks Like

- Recognizing that everyone experiences failure, rejection, or self-doubt at some point.
- Letting go of the belief that your imperfections make you uniquely flawed.

Why It Matters

Isolation amplifies pain, while connection reduces it. When you remember that your struggles are shared by others, you feel less burdened and more supported.

Exercise: The Shared Struggle Reflection

Think about a challenge you're facing right now. Write down one way this struggle connects you to others.

Example:

- Struggle: Feeling like a failure after being rejected for a promotion.

- Connection: Remembering that everyone faces rejection at some point, and it doesn't define their worth, or yours.

3. Mindfulness: Observing Without Judgment

Mindfulness is the practice of being present with your thoughts and feelings without over-identifying with them or pushing them away. It's about creating space to acknowledge what you're experiencing without letting it consume you.

What It Looks Like

- Instead of thinking, *"I'm so overwhelmed, I'll never get through this, "* you observe, *"I'm feeling overwhelmed right now, but this feeling will pass."*

- Instead of avoiding difficult emotions, you sit with them and allow yourself to process them.

Why It Matters

Mindfulness prevents you from getting stuck in cycles of rumination or avoidance. It helps you respond to challenges with clarity and calmness, rather than reactivity or denial.

Exercise: Mindful Journaling

- Take five minutes to write about how you're feeling right now.

- Focus on describing your emotions without judgment. Instead of saying, *"I shouldn't feel this way, "* write, *"I'm noticing that I feel anxious and unsure."*

Example Entry:

- *"I feel disappointed about not reaching my goal, but I'm reminding myself that this feeling doesn't define me. It's okay to feel this way, and I know I'll find a path forward."*

Bringing It All Together

These three elements, self-kindness, common humanity, and mindfulness, work together to create a powerful framework for self-compassion:

- **Self-Kindness** helps you soften your inner critic and approach yourself with care.

- **Common Humanity** reminds you that you're never alone in your struggles.

- **Mindfulness** allows you to experience your emotions without judgment or overwhelm.

Reflection Exercise: Your Self-Compassion Snapshot

Take a moment to reflect on how each element of self-compassion shows up in your life right now:

- How do you practice self-kindness?
- When have you reminded yourself that you're not alone?
- How do you create space to observe your feelings without judgment?

Write down one way you'd like to strengthen each element moving forward.

In the next section, we'll dive into practical steps for incorporating these elements into your daily life, so you can begin experiencing the transformative power of self-compassion for yourself.

Are you ready to start putting these principles into action? Let's continue.

Practical Steps to Practice Radical Self-Compassion

Why Practicing Self-Compassion Matters

Understanding self-compassion is one thing, but putting it into action is where transformation happens. It's in the daily moments, the small choices, and the quiet conversations you have with yourself that the true power of self-compassion takes root.

Why does it matter? Because life will always bring challenges, mistakes, and moments of self-doubt. These exercises aren't just practices, they're lifelines. They're tools to help you break free from the cycle of self-criticism and create a relationship with yourself that is grounded in care, kindness, and resilience.

Think about this: How often have you shown compassion to others, even in their darkest moments? How often have you encouraged a friend or loved one when they felt lost or overwhelmed? You already know how to offer grace and understanding, it's time to give that same gift to yourself.

These steps are not about being perfect or "fixing" yourself, they're about learning to hold space for your own humanity. They're about nurturing the parts of you that have long been silenced by doubt or judgment and giving yourself permission to be exactly who you are.

Each exercise you practice is a step toward freedom, the freedom to embrace your imperfections, to recognize your worth, and to live a life guided by self-acceptance. You are worthy of that freedom. Let's begin.

Step 1: Talk to Yourself Like a Friend

Think of how you would comfort a friend who's struggling. You wouldn't criticize or dismiss their feelings. Instead, you'd listen, reassure, and remind them of their strengths. You deserve that same kindness.

Exercise: Rewrite Negative Self-Talk

- Write down a self-critical thought you've had recently.

    o Example: *"I can't believe I failed at that. I'm so useless."*

- Now, rewrite it as if you were speaking to a friend.

    o Example: *"It's okay to make mistakes. This doesn't define you, and you're still capable of moving forward."*

- Practice saying this rewritten statement to yourself aloud.

Why it matters: This exercise helps reframe your inner dialogue, replacing self-criticism with encouragement and care.

Step 2: Normalize Your Struggles

When life feels hard, it's easy to believe you're the only one going through it. But challenges and setbacks are universal. Reminding yourself of this can reduce feelings of isolation and shame.

Exercise: The "You're Not Alone" Journal

- Write about a recent struggle.
    - Example: *"I felt rejected when I wasn't invited to the event. It made me question my value."*
- Reflect on how this experience connects you to others.
    - Example: *"Everyone experiences rejection at some point. It doesn't mean I'm unworthy, it means I'm human."*
- End with a statement of compassion: *"I'm not alone in this, and I'll be okay."*

Why it matters: Recognizing shared humanity helps you see your struggles as part of life, not a reflection of your inadequacy.

Step 3: Cultivate Mindfulness

Mindfulness allows you to observe your emotions without judgment or overwhelm. It helps you create space to respond with intention rather than reacting out of habit.

Exercise: Emotional Check-In

- Find a quiet space and close your eyes.
- Take a deep breath and ask yourself: *"What am I feeling right now?"*
- Name the emotion without judging it.
    - Example: *"I feel anxious and unsure."*
- Acknowledge the emotion with kindness: "It's okay to feel this way. This feeling will pass."
- Take a few more deep breaths, focusing on the sensation of letting go.

Why it matters: This practice helps you stay present with your emotions, reducing the tendency to suppress or over-identify with them.

Step 4: Write Yourself a Self-Compassion Letter

This powerful exercise combines self-kindness, common humanity, and mindfulness into one reflective practice.

How to Do It

- Think of a situation where you've been hard on yourself.
- Write a letter to yourself from the perspective of someone who loves and supports you unconditionally.
  - Acknowledge the difficulty of the situation.
  - Remind yourself that struggle is part of being human.
  - Offer words of comfort and encouragement.

Example:

"Dear [Your Name],

I know you've been feeling like you're not doing enough lately, and that's been weighing on you. It's okay to feel this way, it means you care. But remember, you're doing the best you can, and that's all anyone can ask of you. You're not alone in this struggle, and it doesn't define your worth. Be gentle with yourself, you deserve it."

Why it matters: This letter becomes a tangible reminder of your capacity for self-compassion.

Step 5: Celebrate Your Imperfections

Perfection isn't attainable, and striving for it often leads to exhaustion and disappointment. Instead, learn to embrace your imperfections as part of what makes you beautifully human.

Exercise: Gratitude for Imperfection

- Think of a recent mistake or shortcoming.
  - Example: *"I forgot an important deadline."*
- Identify one thing you learned or gained from the experience.
  - Example: *"It reminded me to be more mindful of my schedule, and I learned how to ask for help."*
- Write a gratitude statement: "I'm grateful for this experience because it helped me grow."

Why it matters: This exercise shifts your perspective, allowing you to see value in your imperfections rather than fearing them.

Step 6: Commit to a Daily Self-Compassion Practice

Self-compassion isn't a one-time activity, it's a habit. Start small by integrating moments of self-compassion into your daily routine.

Ideas for Daily Practices

- Start each day with an affirmation: *"I am worthy of kindness and care, just as I am."*
- Take a five-minute mindfulness break to check in with your emotions.

- End each day by reflecting on one way you treated yourself with compassion.

Self-compassion is a journey, not a destination. Some days, it will feel natural; other days, it will feel like an uphill climb. But every time you choose kindness over criticism, connection over isolation, and mindfulness over judgment, you strengthen your ability to navigate life's challenges with grace.

In the next section, we'll explore real-life stories of transformation, showing how self-compassion has changed the lives of others, and how it can change yours, too.

Stories of Transformation

Nothing illustrates the power of self-compassion better than real-life stories. Hearing how others have embraced self-compassion can inspire you to take your own steps toward healing and growth. In this section, we'll explore two transformative journeys, Sabrina's and a client's, showing how self-compassion reshaped their lives.

Sabrina's Story: Learning to Offer Herself Grace

After the end of my marriage, I was consumed by self-blame. I replayed every argument, every decision, every moment I thought I could have done better. I convinced myself that if I had been more patient, more understanding, or somehow more *worthy,* things would have been different.

For months, I carried the weight of those thoughts. I struggled to move forward because I felt like I didn't deserve to. Then, one day, a mentor asked me a simple but profound question: *"If a friend came to you with this story, how would you respond?"*

That question stopped me in my tracks. I realized I would never speak to a friend the way I was speaking to myself. I would never tell someone else that they were unworthy of love because of a mistake or failure. Why, then, was I holding myself to such a cruel standard?

From that day forward, I began practicing self-compassion. It wasn't easy. The critical voice in my head didn't disappear overnight. But little by little, I replaced it with a kinder, more understanding voice. I reminded myself that I was human, that my mistakes don't define me, and that I was worthy of grace, even from myself.

That shift didn't just help me heal, it transformed the way I saw myself. It gave me the strength to rebuild my life, not from a place of shame, but from a place of self-acceptance.

A Client's Story: Overcoming the Fear of Failure

One of my clients, Maria, came to me after experiencing what she called "a devastating failure." She had poured her heart into a business venture, only to see it crumble after a few months. She told me, *"I don't think I'll ever recover from this. I feel like a complete failure."*

Maria's inner critic was relentless. It told her she wasn't smart enough, resourceful enough, or resilient enough to succeed. She avoided talking to friends and family because she was so ashamed.

In our sessions, I introduced Maria to the practice of self-compassion. At first, she resisted. She thought being kind to herself meant letting herself off the hook. But over time, she began to see that self-compassion wasn't about excusing her mistakes, it was about learning from them without letting them define her.

One day, I asked Maria to write a letter to herself, imagining she was speaking to a dear friend who had gone through the same experience. At first, she struggled. But as she wrote, her tone softened. She acknowledged how hard she had worked, how much she had learned, and how brave she was for trying in the first place.

By the end of the exercise, Maria was in tears. She said, *"I've never spoken to myself this way before. It feels... freeing."* That moment marked a turning point for her. She began to see her failure not as a reflection of her worth, but as a stepping stone on her journey.

Today, Maria is building a new business, one rooted in the lessons she learned from her first attempt. She tells me, *"I don't let fear of failure stop me anymore. I know I'll be okay no matter what, because I've learned how to be kind to myself."*

Your Story Can Be Next

Mine and Maria's stories are reminders that self-compassion has the power to transform even the most painful experiences. It doesn't erase the challenges you face, but it gives you the strength to face them with grace and resilience.

Think about your own journey. What might shift if you started speaking to yourself with kindness? How might your life change if you embrace your imperfections instead of criticizing them?

You don't have to have it all figured out. You don't have to get it right every time. All you have to do is take one small step toward treating yourself with the care and understanding you deserve.

In the next section, we'll provide practical exercises to help you begin that journey, because your story deserves to be one of healing and growth, too.

Exercises: Self-Compassion Checking

These exercises are designed to help you put self-compassion into practice. They will guide you in replacing self-criticism with kindness, embracing your shared humanity, and cultivating mindfulness in your daily life. Remember, this is not about doing everything perfectly, it's about taking small, intentional steps toward treating yourself with the care and understanding you deserve.

Exercise 1: The Self-Compassion Letter

Purpose: To replace self-criticism with self-kindness and understanding.

Writing a letter to yourself from a compassionate perspective helps you reframe your inner dialogue and process challenging emotions with care.

How to Do It:

- Think of a situation where you've been hard on yourself.
    - Example: A mistake at work, a failed relationship, or feeling overwhelmed by responsibilities.

- Write a letter to yourself as if you were speaking to a dear friend. Use a tone that is kind, supportive, and understanding.
    - Acknowledge the difficulty of the situation.
    - Remind yourself that struggle is a part of being human.
    - Offer words of comfort and encouragement.

- When finished, read the letter aloud to yourself.

Template:

- *"Dear [Your Name],*

- *I know you're feeling [emotion] about [situation], and that's completely understandable. This is a hard moment, and it's okay to feel this way. Remember, you are not alone, everyone faces challenges like this at some point. What matters is that you are showing up, learning, and trying your best. You are worthy of kindness and care, even now. I'm proud of you for [positive action], and I know you'll get through this."*

Exercise 2: The "Pause and Reflect" Practice

Purpose: To cultivate mindfulness and reduce emotional reactivity.

This exercise helps you slow down and process your feelings without judgment, creating space for clarity and compassion.

How to Do It:

- When you notice a strong emotion (like frustration, sadness, or anxiety), pause and take three deep breaths.
- Ask yourself:
  - *"What am I feeling right now?"*
  - *"What do I need at this moment?"*
- Acknowledge your feelings without judgment.
  - *Example: "I'm feeling overwhelmed, and that's okay. This is a tough moment, but it will pass."*
- Offer yourself a small act of care, like a comforting word, a short break, or a deep breath.

Exercise 3: Gratitude for Imperfection

Purpose: To reframe your perception of mistakes and struggles, recognizing their role in your growth.

How to Do It:

- Think of a recent mistake or imperfection that has been bothering you.
- Reflect on what you've learned or gained from this experience.
  - Example: *"Missing that deadline taught me the importance of asking for help sooner."*
- Write a gratitude statement:
  - *"I am grateful for this experience because it helped me grow in [specific way]."*
- Repeat this exercise whenever self-criticism arises.

Exercise 4: The Daily Self-Compassion Check-In

Purpose: To integrate self-compassion into your daily routine.

How to Do It:

- Set aside 5 minutes at the end of each day to reflect on how you treated yourself.
- Ask yourself:
  - "Was I kind to myself today?"
  - "Where could I have been more compassionate?"
  - "What can I do tomorrow to be gentler with myself?"

- Write down one thing you're proud of and one way you'll show yourself kindness tomorrow.

Exercise 5: The Shared Struggle Reflection

Purpose: To embrace common humanity and reduce feelings of isolation during difficult times.

How to Do It:

- Think of a challenge you're currently facing.
- Reflect on how this challenge connects you to others.
  - Example: "Struggling with self-doubt reminds me that everyone feels unsure sometimes. I'm not alone in this."
- Write a short statement affirming your shared humanity:
  - *"This is hard, but I'm not alone. Struggle is part of being human."*

These exercises are tools to help you cultivate self-compassion as a daily practice. They're not about achieving perfection, they're about progress. Start with one or two exercises that resonate with you and build from there. Over time, these practices will help you create a more compassionate relationship with yourself, one rooted in kindness, understanding, and grace.

In the next section, we'll wrap up this chapter with a conclusion that ties together everything you've learned and sets the stage for the rest of your journey.

Becoming Your Own Advocate

As you reach the end of this chapter, pause for a moment and reflect on everything you've explored. You've looked at the weight of self-criticism, the power of self-compassion, and the practical steps to nurture a kinder relationship with yourself. Each concept, exercise, and story shared here has one purpose: to remind you that you are worthy of the same grace and understanding you freely give to others.

Self-compassion isn't about fixing yourself, it's about accepting yourself as you are, flaws and all. It's the radical act of treating yourself with kindness, even on days when you feel like you don't deserve it. When you practice self-compassion, you give yourself the freedom to make mistakes, learn, and grow without fear of judgment.

This is your permission to let go of the impossible standards you've been holding yourself to. To stop measuring your worth by what you achieve or how perfectly you perform. To know that even on your hardest days, you are enough.

When you embrace self-compassion, the benefits ripple outward:

- You become more resilient, able to face challenges without crumbling under the weight of self-doubt.

- Your relationships deepen because you're no longer seeking validation from others to fill the gaps left by your own inner critic.

- Your confidence grows because you trust yourself to handle life's ups and downs with care.

And perhaps most importantly, self-compassion creates space for joy. When you let go of the need to prove yourself, you open your heart to the beauty and fullness of life.

This chapter is just the beginning. Self-compassion isn't something you master overnight, it's a lifelong practice. Some days, it will feel natural and effortless. Other days, you'll have to remind yourself to pause, breathe, and choose kindness over criticism. That's okay. Progress, not perfection, is the goal.

Take what resonates from this chapter and begin integrating it into your life. Start small. Write yourself a compassionate letter. Pause and reflect when emotions feel overwhelming. Celebrate your imperfections as stepping stones to growth. Each step, no matter how small, is a victory.

4: Envisioning a Life Built on Self-Worth

"Daring to Dream: Creating a Life That Reflects Your True Worth"
The Courage to Dream

Imagine looking back on your life five, ten, or even twenty years from now. What would it feel like to realize that you never pursued your dreams because you doubted your worth? The regret of "what if" can be heavy, but here's the good news: you don't have to carry it. Today, you have the power to create a vision for your life that reflects your true worth, a vision that excites you and aligns with the person you're meant to be.

Vision is more than wishful thinking. It's a roadmap that guides your actions, decisions, and energy toward the life you desire. When rooted in self-worth, your vision becomes a powerful tool, not just to dream but to build. It reminds you that you are capable, deserving, and in control of creating a future that fulfills you.

But here's the thing: many of us shy away from envisioning the life we want. We're afraid of dreaming "too big" or "too small." We let external expectations, fear of failure, or feelings of inadequacy hold us back. And in doing so, we rob ourselves of the joy, purpose, and fulfillment that come from living authentically.

This chapter is an invitation to change that. It's about giving yourself permission to dream without limits and to craft a vision that is uniquely yours. Whether your ideal life involves personal achievements, meaningful relationships, or simply waking up each day with peace and purpose, your vision is valid, and it's worth pursuing.

Why Vision Matters

Without a clear vision, it's easy to drift through life, letting circumstances and other people's priorities dictate your path. You might find yourself stuck in a cycle of routine, constantly reacting to what life throws at you instead of actively creating the life you want.

A vision rooted in self-worth changes everything. It gives you direction, purpose, and the confidence to take meaningful steps forward. It also serves as a powerful motivator, reminding you why your efforts matter, especially when challenges arise.

Your vision is only as strong as the foundation it's built on. That foundation is your self-worth, the belief that you are inherently valuable and deserving of the life you envision. Without self-worth, even the most inspiring dreams can feel out of reach. You might downplay your aspirations, settle for less, or abandon your goals altogether.

But when you approach your vision with a deep sense of self-worth, everything shifts. You no longer need external validation to pursue your dreams. You're not afraid to take risks or fail because you know your worth isn't tied to outcomes. Instead, you're empowered to dream boldly, knowing that you have everything you need within you to create a life that feels true and fulfilling.

Crafting a vision isn't about having all the answers right now. It's a process of self-discovery, identifying what truly matters to you, what lights you up, and what aligns with your values. It's about peeling back the layers of societal "shoulds" and getting clear on what *you* want, not what others expect of you.

This journey requires courage. It asks you to dream beyond your current circumstances and to trust in possibilities you can't yet see. But it also offers incredible rewards: clarity, confidence, and the excitement of knowing you're building a life that reflects your worth.

Your Vision Starts Here

In this chapter, you'll learn how to:

- Break free from external expectations to define a vision that feels authentic to you.

- Align your goals with your self-worth so they feel both meaningful and achievable.

- Use visualization techniques to bring your ideal life into focus and fuel your motivation.

- Take actionable steps to move from dreaming to doing.

This isn't about creating a perfect plan, it's about daring to dream and taking the first step. You deserve a life that feels aligned with who you are and what you value. And the best part? The journey to get there starts right now.

So let's begin. Imagine the life you want, not the one you think you're "supposed" to have, but the one that sets your soul on fire. That vision is waiting for you. Let's bring it to life.

Creating Your Vision of a Worthy Life

Let's get one thing straight: your dreams are valid. Yes, *yours*. Not the watered-down version you think is acceptable or achievable, but the full, vibrant, soul-stirring dreams you might not even dare to speak out loud. Somewhere along the way, you may have convinced yourself that your desires are too big, too small, or too "out there." But here's the truth: your vision doesn't need to fit into anyone else's mold, it only needs to fit *you.*

Defining your vision is an act of self-love. It's a declaration that you deserve a life aligned with your values, passions, and deepest joys. It's also a reminder that you're allowed to dream without apology or limitation. So, let's kick self-doubt to the curb and get real about the life you want to create.

1. Letting Go of External Expectations

Raise your hand if you've ever felt like you're living someone else's life. (Okay, you don't actually have to raise your hand, this isn't *that* kind of book, but you get the point.) Maybe you've been chasing goals that don't really excite you or living according to rules you didn't write. It's exhausting, isn't it?

Here's the thing: life is too short to spend it trying to meet expectations that don't even belong to you. Defining your vision starts with letting go of what others think you *should* want and asking yourself what *you* truly desire.

Why This Matters

When you live for someone else's approval, you're giving them the keys to your happiness. But when you choose to honor your own dreams, you're reclaiming those keys and saying, *"I'll drive, thanks."*

Reflection Prompt: Unpacking the Shoulds

Ask yourself:

- What expectations have I been carrying that don't feel authentic to me?

- If I didn't care about judgment or approval, what would I choose for my life?

And remember: Letting go of other people's "shoulds" doesn't mean you're selfish. It means you're brave enough to live your truth.

2. Discovering Your Values and Passions

If you've ever been asked, *"What are you passionate about?"* and immediately felt like you had to say something profound, don't worry, you're not alone. (Pro tip: Your passion doesn't have to be saving the planet or discovering a cure for something. It could be as simple as baking cookies that make people smile or watching a sunset in perfect silence. Both are equally valid.)

At its core, your vision is a reflection of your values, the principles that matter most to you, and your passions, those things that light you up inside.

Why This Matters

When you align your life with your values and passions, you're not just existing, you're thriving. You're creating a life that feels authentic and fulfilling because it's built around what truly matters to you.

Reflection Prompt: What Makes Your Soul Sing?

- What are the three qualities you admire most in yourself or others? (Kindness? Creativity? Adventure?)

- When was the last time you felt completely at peace or energized? What were you doing?

Let's be real, if your passion is binge-watching rom-coms while eating pizza, own it. Who says your dream life can't include Netflix and extra cheese? You're building a life for *you*, not auditioning for a Hallmark movie.

3. Dreaming Without Limits: Unleashing the Life You Deserve

Take a moment and think back to when you were a child. Remember those wild, uninhibited dreams you had? Maybe you wanted to be an astronaut, a famous artist, or someone who discovered new worlds. There were no limits, no second-guessing, and definitely no voices in your head saying, *"That's not realistic."* You dreamed without fear because, back then, the world felt limitless. What if you could dream that way again?

As adults, we've been trained to downplay our aspirations. We tell ourselves to be "practical" or "realistic." But here's a truth that no one talks about enough: **The only dreams that are truly unrealistic are the ones you don't allow yourself to have.**

Dreaming without limits doesn't mean ignoring reality, it means expanding your reality. It's about giving yourself permission to envision a life that aligns with your deepest desires, not just what feels safe or acceptable. It's about looking past the "how" and focusing on the "what" and "why." The *how* can come later; for now, let's focus on daring to dream.

Why Do We Hold Back?

Let's get real. Why is it so hard for us to dream freely?

- Fear of Failure
  - "What if I go after this and it doesn't work out?"
  - Failure isn't the opposite of success, it's part of the process. Every great achievement starts with someone who dared to try.
- Fear of Judgment
  - "What will people think of me?"
  - People will always have opinions, but they don't have to define your choices. You're the one living your life, not them.
- Feelings of Unworthiness
  - "Do I even deserve this?"
  - Yes, you do. Your worth isn't something you have to earn, it's inherent. If your dream lights you up, it's valid, and you are worthy of pursuing it.

The Power of a Limitless Dream

Dreaming without limits is transformative because it:

- Expands Possibilities: When you remove self-imposed restrictions, you open yourself to opportunities you may never have considered.

- Clarifies Priorities: Your dreams reveal what truly matters to you, your passions, values, and deepest desires.

- Fuels Motivation: A dream that excites you gives you the energy and drive to take action, even when challenges arise.

Exercise: The "Magic Wand" Visualization

Let's put fear and doubt aside for a moment and step into a world where anything is possible.

- Close Your Eyes and Imagine:

- You've been handed a magic wand that can create your perfect life. There are no limitations, no financial constraints, no fears, no rules. As you wave the wand, imagine:

  - Where are you waking up? What does the space around you look like?

  - How do you feel as you start your day? Energized? Peaceful? Excited?

  - What are you doing? Are you pursuing a passion? Leading a meaningful project? Traveling the world?

  - Who is with you? What are your relationships like?

- Write It Down:

- Take 10 minutes to write a detailed description of this dream life. Be as specific as possible, describe the sights, sounds, emotions, and experiences.

- Ask Yourself:

  - *What about this vision feels most exciting to me?*

  - *What values does this dream reflect?*

- Reflect Without Judgment:

- Look at what you've written and allow yourself to feel the joy and possibility of it. This isn't about figuring out how to make it happen yet, it's about reconnecting with your capacity to dream.

Addressing the "What Ifs"

Dreaming big can bring up all kinds of "what if" thoughts: *What if I fail? What if I'm not good enough? What if it's too late?* Let's flip those questions:

- What if you succeed beyond your wildest imagination?

- What if you discover strength and resilience you never knew you had?

- What if your dream life is closer than you think, just waiting for you to take the first step?

The only way to know is to try. Dreams are like seeds, they need nurturing, patience, and belief to grow. And yes, not every seed will flourish, but every step you take toward your dream teaches you something valuable.

Your dreams don't have to be traditional or grand to matter. If your vision involves owning a cat sanctuary, writing fantasy novels from a cozy cabin, or becoming a professional pasta taste-tester, go for it. (Seriously, who wouldn't want to taste-test pasta for a living?) Your dreams are an expression of your unique self, and that makes them worth pursuing.

Your Dream, Your Permission

Here's the most important part: You don't need anyone else's permission to dream big. You don't need the world to agree with you or validate your vision. The only person who needs to believe in your dream is *you*.

Dreaming without limits is an act of self-love and courage. It's a way of saying to yourself, *"I am worthy of more. I deserve to create a life that lights me up."*

So, let's stop asking, *"Is this possible?"* and start asking, *"What if it is?"* Your dreams are waiting. Are you ready to step into them?

Aligning Your Vision with Your True Self

Here's where the magic happens. Once you've defined what you want, it's time to align it with who you are at your core. Your vision should reflect your authentic self, not the version of you that's trying to please others or meet impossible standards.

Why This Matters

When your vision aligns with your true self, it feels right. You're not chasing a life you think you *should* have, you're creating a life that feels deeply meaningful and fulfilling.

Reflection Prompt: Anchoring in Authenticity

- Does my vision reflect my values, or am I still holding onto external expectations?
- How does my dream life honor who I am and what I believe in?

Defining your vision isn't about perfection, it's about authenticity. It's about daring to ask yourself, *"What do I really want?"* and giving yourself permission to go after it.

You don't have to have all the answers right now. Dreams evolve, and so will your vision. The important thing is to start. Because here's the truth: You are deserving of the life you imagine, no matter how big, small, or unconventional it may seem.

So take a deep breath. Let go of the "shoulds." Embrace your passions. And dream without limits. Your vision is waiting for you, it's time to claim it.

Aligning Your Vision with Self-Worth

You've taken a brave step by daring to dream and defining your vision. But now comes an equally important part: aligning your vision with your self-worth. Your dreams might be vivid, inspiring, and exciting, but they can only become reality when rooted in the belief that *you are deserving of them.*

Let's be honest, self-doubt has a sneaky way of creeping in just when you start to imagine a brighter, bolder future. You might find yourself asking:

- *"Do I really deserve this life?"*
- *"Am I capable of achieving these dreams?"*
- *"What if I'm not enough?"*

Here's the truth: Your self-worth is not something you earn by achieving your dreams; it's the foundation that makes pursuing those dreams possible. When you align your vision with the unshakable belief in your own value, you give yourself the freedom to chase your goals without fear or hesitation.

Why Self-Worth Matters in Realizing Your Vision

Imagine building a house on unstable ground. No matter how beautiful the design, the structure will eventually crumble because its foundation isn't strong enough to support it. Your dreams are no different. Without self-worth as the foundation, you might:

- Downplay your aspirations, settling for a life that feels "safe" but unfulfilling.

- Abandon your vision at the first sign of failure, believing it was never meant for you.

- Pursue goals for external validation, leaving you feeling empty even if you succeed.

But when your vision is rooted in self-worth, you approach it with confidence and resilience. You're not chasing your dreams to prove your value, you're chasing them because you already know you're worthy of living a life that lights you up.

The Fear of Dreaming "Too Big" or "Too Small"

Many of us struggle with the size of our dreams.

- Dreaming "too big" can feel overwhelming, like we're setting ourselves up for disappointment.

- Dreaming "too small" can feel underwhelming, as though we're not allowing ourselves to aim for something meaningful.

But here's the truth: There's no such thing as the "right" size for your dreams. What matters is that your vision feels authentic to you.

Reflection Prompt: What Feels Right for Me?

Ask yourself:

- Does this vision excite me and feel aligned with who I am?
- Am I pursuing this dream because it's meaningful to me, or because I think it's what I'm supposed to want?

Your dreams don't have to impress anyone else. They only need to resonate with *you*.

One of the biggest barriers to aligning your vision with self-worth is the belief that you're not enough, *not smart enough, talented enough, or deserving enough.* This mindset can keep you stuck, afraid to take even the first step toward your dreams.

Let's rewrite that story.

Why You Are Already Enough

- You don't need to have all the answers to begin. Every expert was once a beginner.
- Your worth isn't tied to your accomplishments, it's inherent, simply because you exist.
- Pursuing your dreams is an act of courage and growth, not a measure of perfection.

Exercise: Rewriting Your Inner Narrative

- Write down a self-doubt statement that's been holding you back.
    - Example: *"I'm not talented enough to achieve this."*

- Replace it with a statement of self-worth.
  - Example: *"I may not have all the skills yet, but I am capable of learning and growing. I deserve to pursue this dream."*

- Repeat this new narrative daily, especially when doubt creeps in.

Aligning with Your Personal Truth

Your vision should reflect your personal truths, not society's expectations, not your parents' dreams for you, not what your friends are doing. It should be rooted in what feels meaningful and fulfilling to you.

Reflection Prompt: Returning to Authenticity

- What parts of my vision feel most true to who I am?

- Are there elements of my vision that I've included out of obligation rather than desire?

When your vision aligns with your authentic self, it becomes a source of joy and inspiration rather than pressure.

How Self-Worth Fuels Action

Aligning your vision with self-worth doesn't just shift your mindset, it also drives your actions. When you believe in your own value, you're more likely to:

- Take bold steps toward your goals, even when they feel challenging.

- Seek opportunities and resources that support your dreams.

- Persevere through setbacks, knowing they don't define your worth.

Exercise: Your Worthy Action Plan

- Write down one part of your vision that excites you the most.
  - Example: *"I want to start my own business."*
- Identify one small step you can take toward that dream this week.
  - Example: *"Research online courses or resources that can help me get started."*
- Celebrate every action you take, no matter how small. Each step is a victory in living out your worth.

Your dreams are not too big, too small, or too far away. They are reflections of your inner truth, and they are achievable when you align them with the unshakable belief that you are deserving of them.

You don't have to have all the answers right now. You don't have to know exactly how your vision will come to life. All you need is the courage to believe in your worth and take one step forward.

As we move into the next section, we'll explore the power of visualization and how it can help bring your vision to life. Get ready to see your dreams with new clarity and motivation!

The Process of Visualization

Visualization is more than just daydreaming, it's a powerful tool for turning your dreams into reality. When you vividly imagine the life you want, you're not just creating a mental picture; you're rewiring your brain to believe in the possibility of that future. This practice helps you align your thoughts, emotions, and actions with your vision, giving you the clarity and motivation needed to move forward.

The Science Behind Visualization

You've likely heard the phrase, *"What you focus on grows."* There's science behind this idea. Visualization activates the brain's **reticular activating system (RAS)**, the network that filters information and helps you focus on what's most important. When you visualize your goals regularly, your brain starts seeking out opportunities and solutions that align with that vision.

Additionally, studies show that visualization stimulates the same neural pathways as actual experiences. In other words, your brain can't fully distinguish between vividly imagining a scenario and living it. This is why elite athletes, successful entrepreneurs, and high achievers across industries use visualization to prepare for success.

Why Visualization Matters for Your Vision

Without a clear picture of what you're working toward, it's easy to lose focus or motivation. Visualization helps you:

- **Clarify Your Goals**: By imagining the details of your vision, you gain a deeper understanding of what you truly want.
- **Build Confidence**: Seeing yourself succeed in your mind boosts your belief in your ability to achieve it.
- **Stay Motivated**: Visualization keeps your dreams alive, even during challenging times.

Think of visualization as your mental rehearsal. The more you practice seeing your dream life, the more natural and achievable it begins to feel.

How to Visualize Effectively

Visualization is most impactful when it's vivid, emotional, and consistent. Here's a step-by-step guide to get started:

1. Create a Quiet Space

Find a quiet, comfortable spot where you can focus without distractions. This is your time to connect with your vision.

2. Engage Your Senses

Close your eyes and imagine your ideal life. Picture it in as much detail as possible:

- **Sight**: What does your environment look like? Are you in a sunny kitchen, a bustling office, or a serene garden?

- **Sound**: What do you hear? The laughter of loved ones? The hum of a city? Birds singing?

- **Touch**: How does it feel to be in this space? Warm sunlight on your skin? A soft chair beneath you?

- **Smell**: Are there scents in the air? Freshly brewed coffee? Flowers?

- **Emotion**: Most importantly, how do you feel? Joyful? Peaceful? Accomplished?

The more senses you involve, the more real and compelling your vision becomes.

3. Anchor Yourself in the Emotion

Pay close attention to how achieving your vision makes you feel. Emotions are the fuel that drives action. Let the joy, pride, or excitement you imagine motivate you to take steps toward making your dream a reality.

4. Focus on the Journey, Not Just the Destination

While it's important to visualize the end goal, also imagine the steps you'll take to get there. See yourself tackling challenges, learning, and growing along the way. This makes your vision feel achievable and prepares your mind for the effort it requires.

5. Make It a Daily Practice

Consistency is key. Spend 5-10 minutes each day visualizing your ideal life. Morning and bedtime are great times to practice, as your mind is more receptive during these moments.

Exercise: Write Your Vision Script

Take your visualization one step further by putting it into words. A vision script is a written narrative of your dream life, described as if you're already living it.

How to Write Your Vision Script

- Start with the phrase, "I am so grateful to be living a life where…"

- Write in the present tense, as though everything you desire is already happening.

  - Example: *"I am so grateful to wake up each morning in my peaceful home. I feel energized and excited to work on projects that align with my passions. I am surrounded by people who uplift and inspire me. My days are filled with joy, purpose, and growth."*

- Read your vision script daily, allowing yourself to feel the emotions it evokes.

Addressing Doubt During Visualization

It's normal for doubt or negative thoughts to arise during visualization, especially if your dream feels far away. When this happens:

- **Acknowledge the Doubt**: Don't push it away; instead, observe it without judgment.

- **Reaffirm Your Worth**: Remind yourself, *"I am capable of creating this life because I am worthy of it."*

- **Refocus on the Vision**: Gently bring your attention back to the positive emotions and imagery of your dream life.

The Power of Speaking Your Vision

In addition to visualizing, speak your vision aloud. Hearing yourself describe your goals reinforces your belief in them and strengthens your commitment. This could be as simple as sharing your dreams with a trusted friend or saying daily affirmations like:

- *"I am creating a life I love, filled with joy and purpose."*

- *"I am worthy of every opportunity that comes my way."*

Visualization is more than a mental exercise, it's a declaration of belief in your ability to create the life you deserve. By imagining your dream life with clarity and conviction, you're taking the first step toward making it real.

In the next section, we'll explore how to turn these visualizations into tangible action, one step at a time. Let's bring your vision to life!

Living with Intention and Purpose

Your vision is clear, your heart is full, and the excitement of what's possible is alive in you. Now it's time to move forward and make it real. But where do you begin? How do you turn an inspiring idea into actionable steps? The key lies in starting small, staying consistent, and trusting the process.

In this section, we'll delve deeper into what it takes to bridge the gap between where you are and where you want to be. Along the way, we'll ground the inspiration with data, wisdom, and practical strategies to keep you motivated.

Renowned Chinese philosopher Lao Tzu said, *"The journey of a thousand miles begins with a single step."* It's a phrase we've heard countless times, but its truth is profound. That first step, no matter how small, holds the power to transform dreams into reality.

The Science of Starting Small

Research in psychology shows that breaking down large goals into smaller, manageable tasks increases the likelihood of success. A study published in the *American Journal of Lifestyle Medicine* found that individuals who set small, incremental goals were 63% more likely to maintain progress than those who tackled a large, undefined goal all at once.

When you start small, you remove the mental barriers of overwhelm and fear. Each small win boosts your confidence and builds momentum, creating a positive cycle of action and achievement.

1. Break Down Your Vision into Manageable Goals

A common reason people hesitate to act on their dreams is the sheer size of the vision. You might look at the big picture and think, *"How can I possibly get there?"* The solution is simple: break it down.

How to Do It

- Identify Key Areas: Divide your vision into major categories, such as career, relationships, health, or personal growth.
  - Example: If your vision includes starting a business, create categories like education, networking, finances, and branding.
- Set Specific Milestones: For each category, define tangible, achievable goals.
  - Instead of "get healthier," try "add one vegetable to each meal this week."
  - Instead of "start a business," try "research three potential business ideas by Friday."
- Create a Timeline: Set realistic deadlines for each milestone. This helps you stay accountable and track progress.

Example: From Vision to Action

- **Vision**: Write and publish a book.
- **Breakdown**:
  - Week 1: Brainstorm chapter ideas.

- Week 2: Outline the book.
- Month 1: Write the first chapter.

"You don't have to see the whole staircase, just take the first step." – Martin Luther King Jr.

2. Focus on the Power of One Small Step

When you feel overwhelmed, remind yourself that you don't need to tackle everything at once. Focus on the next small step in front of you. Small actions compound over time, creating significant results.

The Compound Effect

Author Darren Hardy, in his book *The Compound Effect*, explains how small, consistent actions lead to exponential growth. Whether it's saving a little money each week or dedicating 15 minutes a day to a new skill, the impact grows over time.

Actionable Steps

- Daily Progress: Dedicate 10–15 minutes daily to your goal.
  - Example: Spend 15 minutes researching a new career path or journaling ideas for your vision.
- Micro-Commitments: Set tiny, specific goals you can achieve today.
  - Example: Instead of "exercise more, " commit to doing five squats while brushing your teeth.

"Small deeds done are better than great deeds planned." – Peter Marshall

3. Addressing Fear: The Courage to Begin

Fear is a natural response when stepping into the unknown. It whispers, *"What if you fail? What if you're not good enough?"* But here's the truth: Fear doesn't have to disappear for you to move forward. You can act despite it.

How to Overcome Fear

- Reframe Failure: Instead of viewing failure as an endpoint, see it as a stepping stone.
    - Statistic: According to a study by the University of Scranton, people who fail and adjust their approach are 25% more likely to achieve their goals.
- Start Small: Fear shrinks when you take tiny, manageable steps.
    - Example: If the idea of changing careers feels overwhelming, start by reaching out to one person in your desired field for advice.
- Focus on Your Why: Connect with the deeper reason behind your vision.
    - Ask yourself: *"What's at stake if I don't pursue this dream?"*

Remember, you don't need to have it all figured out. Even the world's most successful people started somewhere. Oprah wasn't born Oprah, she started as a local news anchor!

4. Build a Supportive Environment

Your environment shapes your ability to take action. The people, spaces, and habits in your life can either propel you forward or hold you back.

How to Create Support

Surround Yourself with Positive Influences: Connect with people who believe in your vision and encourage your growth.

- Statistic: A Harvard study found that individuals with supportive networks were 47% more likely to achieve their goals.
- Remove Energy Drainers: Limit time with people or activities that drain your motivation.
- Design Your Space for Success: Create a physical environment that inspires action.
  - Example: If you're writing a book, set up a cozy, distraction-free corner with all your tools ready.

5. Celebrate Every Win

Every step forward, no matter how small, is worth celebrating. Acknowledging your progress reinforces positive habits and keeps you motivated.

Why Celebrate?

- Boosts Confidence: Celebrating small wins signals to your brain that you're on the right track.
- Reinforces Progress: It reminds you that each step matters.

How to Celebrate

- Personal Rewards: Treat yourself to something meaningful, a quiet evening, your favorite dessert, or a new journal.
- Reflect and Share: Write about your progress in a journal or share it with a supportive friend.

"Success is the sum of small efforts, repeated day in and day out." – Robert Collier

Exercise: The First Step Commitment

- Define One Small Step
  - Write down one specific action you'll take in the next 24 hours.
    - Example: "I'll research three free online courses related to my vision."

Anchor It with Affirmation

- Write a positive statement to motivate yourself:
  - "Every small step I take is a victory that brings me closer to my dreams."

Set a Time

- Commit to a specific time to complete your step.

Celebrate Completion

- Once you've taken the step, celebrate! Reflect on how it feels to be in motion.

Taking the first step is an act of courage. It signals to the universe, and to yourself, that you're serious about creating a life aligned with your vision. Remember, progress matters more than perfection. Every step, no matter how small, is proof that you're moving forward.

As you continue this journey, know that you're not alone. In the next section, we'll explore real-life stories of transformation to inspire you and remind you that your vision is possible.

Stories of Transformation: Real-Life Proof of What's Possible

When you're at the start of a transformative journey, it's easy to feel alone. You might wonder, *"Can I really do this? Can someone like me achieve this vision?"* The answer is a resounding yes. Throughout history and even in our everyday lives, countless people have turned their dreams into reality by taking intentional steps, facing their fears, and believing in their worth.

In this section, you'll read stories of individuals, including Sabrina's personal journey and testimonials from her clients, who embraced the process of change. These stories are a testament to the power of vision, self-worth, and persistence.

My Story: Rising from the Ashes

2019 was the year my life fell apart, or at least, that's how it felt at the time. My marriage, which I had once believed was unshakable, was hanging on by a thread. Self-doubt crept into every corner of my mind, whispering fears and insecurities that I couldn't silence. On the surface, I was keeping it all together, but inside, I was overwhelmed, lost, and unsure of how to move forward.

It wasn't just about my marriage. It was about something deeper. I had spent so much time trying to be what others needed me to be that I had lost sight of my own worth. I had been pouring into everyone else's cup while my own sat empty. But as the cracks in my world grew bigger, I began to realize that this wasn't just the end of something, it could be the beginning of something new.

The Night Everything Changed

I'll never forget the night that forced me to confront the truth. It was a moment of heartbreak, yes, but it was also a moment of clarity. I was standing there, holding onto the pieces of a life I thought I wanted, and I realized something that would change everything: *I deserved better.*

Not just better from my marriage or my circumstances, I deserved better from *myself.*

Looking back, that night was the turning point. Through the pain, anger, and fear, I discovered a strength I didn't even know I had. I remember looking at myself in the mirror and thinking, *"You can't keep waiting for someone else to save you. It's time to save yourself."*

It wasn't about blaming anyone else or pretending the pain wasn't real. It was about deciding, in that moment, to reclaim my life and my worth.

Step by Step, I Chose Myself

The journey wasn't easy. Healing never is. But I made a decision that night to face the pain head-on and rebuild my life one step at a time.

I started small. I immersed myself in self-reflection, asking hard questions about what I truly wanted and what had been holding me back. I surrounded myself with voices of support, books, mentors, friends, anything that reminded me of my inherent worth. Slowly, I began to define a vision for my future, not based on anyone else's expectations, but on what I deeply desired.

It wasn't perfect. There were moments of doubt and setbacks along the way. But with every small victory, I felt stronger. I began to see my struggles not as obstacles but as opportunities to grow.

Rediscovering My Purpose

One of the most profound lessons I learned on this journey was that my worth wasn't tied to my circumstances, achievements, or relationships. It wasn't something I had to earn or prove. My worth was already within me, it always had been.

As I rebuilt my life, I started to see the bigger picture. My experiences, as painful as they were, had shaped me into someone who could help others. My journey wasn't just about finding peace, it was about finding purpose. I realized that the tools and lessons I had discovered could be shared with others who were feeling lost, stuck, or unworthy.

Why I Wrote This Book

Today, my life looks completely different. I've rebuilt my confidence, redefined my vision, and created a life that aligns with my values and passions. But more importantly, I've committed myself to helping others do the same.

This book is an extension of my journey. It's filled with the insights, strategies, and tools that helped me transform my life from one of self-doubt to one of self-worth. I want you to know that no matter where you're starting from, no matter how heavy your burdens feel, change is possible.

I'm not sharing this story because I have all the answers or because my life is perfect. I'm sharing it because I've been where you are, questioning whether things can ever get better. And I'm here to tell you, they can.

This book is your roadmap to rediscovering your worth, reclaiming your vision, and taking the steps to create the life you deserve. If I could do it, so can you.

Client Success Stories: The Ripple Effect of Transformation

As I began my journey toward healing and self-worth, I realized that my story wasn't unique. Many people, especially women, struggle with self-doubt, broken relationships, and unfulfilled dreams. That's why I chose to dedicate my work to helping others navigate their own paths to transformation.

Over the years, I've had the privilege of guiding incredible individuals through their journeys. Their stories are living proof that with the right tools, mindset, and belief in oneself, profound change is possible. Here are a few of those stories, shared with their permission, to inspire and remind you that you're not alone in this process.

1. Rediscovering Confidence: Sarah's Story

When Sarah came to me, she was struggling with imposter syndrome. Despite her many accomplishments, she constantly doubted her abilities and felt like a fraud in her own career. She worried that any day now, someone would "find out" that she wasn't good enough.

Through our coaching, Sarah began to identify the triggers that fueled her self-doubt. We worked on affirmations, visualization exercises, and strategies to reframe her negative thoughts.

Her Breakthrough

- Sarah learned to replace self-critical thoughts with empowering beliefs.

- She created a daily affirmation routine, reminding herself of her strengths and achievements.

- She started celebrating her small wins, which built her confidence over time.

Within months, Sarah applied for a promotion she once thought was out of her reach, and she got it. Today, she's thriving as a leader in her field.

Sarah shared this with me:

"Sabrina helped me see what I couldn't see in myself. Her guidance didn't just boost my confidence; it transformed the way I approach challenges. I feel capable, worthy, and unstoppable."

2. Breaking Free from Toxic Patterns: Maria's Story

Maria had a long history of unhealthy relationships. She often found herself with partners who didn't respect her boundaries, leaving her feeling drained and unworthy of love. When we began working together, Maria admitted that she didn't fully believe she deserved better.

We started by exploring her values and helping her define what a healthy, fulfilling relationship looked like. Maria journaled about past patterns, identified red flags she had overlooked, and began setting boundaries in all areas of her life, not just in romantic relationships.

Her Breakthrough

- Maria practiced daily affirmations about her worth and value.

- She visualized the qualities of a loving, respectful partner and used this vision to guide her decisions.

- She ended a toxic relationship and eventually found a partnership rooted in mutual respect and support.

Maria's words still resonate with me:

"I didn't think I could break the cycle. But Sabrina showed me that it starts with self-love. For the first time, I feel like I'm in a relationship where I'm seen, valued, and respected."

3. Embracing Radical Change: Jasmine's Story

Jasmine always dreamed of starting her own business, but fear held her back. She doubted her ability to succeed and worried about what others would think if she failed. For years, she stayed in a career that felt safe but unfulfilling.

When we began working together, I encouraged Jasmine to take small, manageable steps toward her dream. We focused on breaking her big goal into achievable milestones and reframing her fear of failure as a learning opportunity.

Her Breakthrough

- Jasmine started with simple actions, like researching business ideas and taking online courses.

- She created a vision board to keep her goals visible and inspiring.
- Over time, she gained the confidence to launch her business, and it's now thriving.

Jasmine's testimonial captures her transformation:

"Sabrina's coaching gave me the courage to step out of my comfort zone. She helped me see that my dream wasn't just possible, it was worth pursuing. Now, I wake up every day excited for the life I've created."

Common Threads in Transformation

What ties these stories together? Each of these women:

- **Recognized Their Worth**: They began by challenging the beliefs that held them back.
- **Defined Their Vision**: They gained clarity about what they truly wanted.
- **Took Action**: They started small, stayed consistent, and trusted the process.
- **Stayed Resilient**: They faced challenges but didn't let setbacks define their journeys.

These stories are more than examples, they're reminders that transformation is possible for anyone, including you. If these women could overcome their doubts, fears, and limitations, so can you.

As we move forward, I encourage you to reflect on these journeys and ask yourself:

- What's holding me back from my own transformation?

- What small step can I take today to move closer to the life I deserve?

Remember, your story is still being written. Let's take the next step together.

Turning Inspiration into Action

The stories you've read are inspiring, but inspiration alone won't transform your life, it's action that makes the difference. These exercises are designed to help you reflect on the lessons from this chapter, connect them to your own journey, and take meaningful steps toward your vision.

Exercise 1: Identifying Your Worth

Each transformation story began with a recognition of self-worth. Now it's your turn.

- Reflection Prompt:
  - Write down three qualities that make you unique and valuable.
  - Think about compliments you've received or moments when you felt proud of yourself.
- Affirmation Practice:
  - Create a daily affirmation based on these qualities. For example, *"I am resilient, compassionate, and creative. My worth is undeniable."*
  - Repeat this affirmation each morning to start your day with confidence.

Exercise 2: Mapping Your Vision

Like Jasmine and Sarah, you need a clear vision to guide your actions.

- Visualization:
  - Close your eyes and imagine your ideal life. Think about where you live, what you do, and how you feel.
  - Picture yourself overcoming challenges and achieving your goals.
- Action Plan:
  - Write down one part of your vision that excites you the most.
  - Break it into three actionable steps you can take this week.

Exercise 3: Recognizing Patterns

Maria's breakthrough came from identifying unhealthy patterns in her relationships. This exercise will help you do the same in your life.

- Journaling Prompt:
  - Reflect on past situations where you felt stuck or undervalued (e.g., relationships, career, personal goals).
  - Ask yourself: What beliefs or habits contributed to these experiences?
- Reframing Exercise:
  - Write down one limiting belief you've held about yourself.

- Replace it with an empowering belief. For example:
  - Limiting belief: *"I always fail."*
  - Empowering belief: *"Every step I take teaches me something valuable. I am capable of growth and success."*

Exercise 4: Taking the First Step

Action is the bridge between inspiration and transformation.

- Set a Micro-Goal:
  - Identify one small step you can take today to move closer to your vision.
  - It could be researching something, reaching out to a mentor, or journaling your thoughts.
- Celebrate Your Progress:
  - Once you've completed the step, acknowledge your effort. Write down how it felt to take action.

Owning Your Vision

Envisioning a better life takes courage. It requires you to look beyond the present and believe in a future where you are living fully and authentically. This act of dreaming isn't just an escape, it's a declaration of hope and possibility. It's a promise to yourself that you deserve more, and you are capable of creating it.

Throughout this chapter, you've explored the power of dreaming without limits, aligning your vision with your worth, and taking intentional steps toward transformation. But dreaming alone isn't enough. To truly own your vision, you must commit to it with unwavering belief and consistent action.

Choosing to believe in your vision can feel risky. What if it doesn't work out? What if it takes longer than you expected? These fears are valid, but they should never stop you. Courage isn't the absence of fear, it's the decision to move forward despite it.

By daring to dream, you've already taken the first step. You've given yourself permission to imagine something better. Now, it's about carrying that vision forward, even when the path gets difficult.

Reflection Prompt

- Ask yourself: What would my life look like if I fully committed to my vision? What's at stake if I don't?

Committing to Your Vision

Commitment is a daily choice. It's not about waiting for motivation or the perfect moment, it's about showing up for yourself every day, even in small ways. Your vision doesn't require perfection; it requires persistence.

When you commit to your vision, you're sending a powerful message to yourself: *I believe in my worth, and I'm willing to do the work to honor it.*

Practical Commitment Steps

- **Create a Routine**: Dedicate time each day to work on your vision, whether it's journaling, researching, or taking actionable steps.
- **Celebrate Progress**: Acknowledge even the smallest victories, they are proof of your commitment.

- **Stay Connected to Your Why**: Remind yourself regularly why this vision matters to you.

At the heart of your vision lies your self-worth. Without it, even the brightest dreams can feel out of reach. But when you root your vision in the belief that you are deserving and capable, you give it the foundation to thrive.

Remember:

- Your worth isn't tied to your achievements or circumstances.
- You don't need anyone else's permission to dream big.
- You are enough, exactly as you are, to create the life you envision.

"You are worthy of the life you can't stop dreaming about. Trust your vision, it's leading you to where you're meant to be."

5: Living Your Self-Worth Every Day

Transforming Belief into Action
The Practice of Living Self-Worth

There's a moment in every journey of transformation when you realize something profound: self-worth isn't just a belief, it's a way of life. It's not enough to know you are valuable; you must show yourself, day after day, that you believe it. Living self-worth is about taking the love, respect, and compassion you deserve and weaving them into the fabric of your everyday life.

But here's the truth: living self-worth isn't always easy. Life has a way of challenging you, making you doubt yourself, or convincing you that you're too busy to prioritize your own needs. You might find yourself pushing your boundaries to please others, sacrificing your health for deadlines, or settling for relationships that don't reflect your value. These moments aren't failures, they're invitations. Invitations to pause, reflect, and choose yourself again.

The Courage to Show Up for Yourself

Living self-worth requires courage. It's a radical act to say, *"I matter, and I will act accordingly."* It's not about being selfish; it's about recognizing that when you honor your worth, you show up as your best self for the people and dreams that matter most to you.

Think about it: how often do you pour your energy into others without stopping to refill your own cup? How many times have you ignored your needs because you felt guilty for putting yourself first?

It's time to rewrite that narrative. Living self-worth isn't indulgent, it's essential.

"You owe yourself the love that you so freely give to others." – Unknown

Why Living Self-Worth Transforms Everything

When you start living your self-worth, everything changes. It's not just about feeling better, it's about creating a life that reflects the truth of who you are. It's about choosing actions that affirm your value, even when it's hard.

The Ripple Effect of Living Self-Worth

- **Stronger Relationships**: When you value yourself, you naturally attract people who value you too. You'll find it easier to let go of toxic connections and nurture relationships that are rooted in mutual respect.

- **Improved Mental and Physical Health**: When you care for yourself, your mind and body respond with gratitude. Prioritizing rest, nutrition, and emotional well-being becomes second nature.

- **Unshakable Confidence**: Each intentional choice you make reinforces the belief that you are worthy. Over time, this belief becomes your foundation.

Living self-worth isn't just about changing your life, it's about changing how you show up in the world. When you treat yourself with the love and respect you deserve, you set a powerful example for others to do the same.

From Knowing to Doing

It's easy to understand self-worth in theory. You've heard the affirmations, the motivational quotes, the well-meaning advice: *"You are enough."* But knowing your worth and living it are two very different things.

Living self-worth bridges the gap between belief and action. It's the difference between saying, *"I deserve rest,"* and actually allowing yourself to take a guilt-free nap. It's the difference between recognizing toxic patterns and making the brave decision to break them.

Each day presents a choice: to either act in alignment with your worth or fall back into habits that diminish it. The more you choose self-worth, the more natural it becomes.

Reflection Prompt

- Ask yourself: *What would my life look like if I consistently treated myself like someone who matters?*

What to Expect in This Chapter

This chapter is an invitation to bring your self-worth to life. Together, we'll explore how to:

- Make daily choices that honor your value.
- Set boundaries that protect your energy and well-being.
- Nurture your mind, body, and spirit as acts of love.
- Face challenges like self-doubt, guilt, and fear with resilience.
- Build habits and routines that align with the life you truly deserve.

This isn't about being perfect or transforming overnight. It's about taking small, consistent steps that lead to profound change. Each choice, no matter how small, is an opportunity to affirm your worth.

As we move through this chapter, I want you to hold one truth close: *You are worth every effort you make for yourself.* You don't need to prove it, earn it, or justify it. Your worth simply is.

Let this chapter be a guide, a reminder that living self-worth is a daily practice, a powerful declaration, and a gift you give to yourself and the world.

You're not just reading this chapter, you're stepping into a new way of living. Let's take the first step together.

Self-Worth in Action: Everyday Choices

Self-worth is not just a belief you carry in your heart, it's a practice that shows up in the choices you make every single day. It's reflected in how you treat yourself, how you allow others to treat you, and the priorities you set for your time and energy. Living your self-worth isn't about grand gestures or perfection, it's about the small, intentional actions that align with your value.

The Power of Small Decisions

Every decision, no matter how small, carries the potential to affirm or diminish your worth. Choosing to rest when you're tired, setting a boundary with a demanding colleague, or saying no to something that drains your energy are all acts of self-worth. These choices may feel uncomfortable at first, especially if you've spent years putting others before yourself, but each one is a step toward living the life you deserve.

Reflection

- Think about the last decision you made that prioritized your well-being. How did it feel?

"It's not the mountains ahead to climb that wear you out; it's the pebble in your shoe." – Muhammad Ali

This quote reminds us that it's often the small, unaddressed choices that weigh us down. Living self-worth means paying attention to those "pebbles" and making choices that honor your value.

Examples of Self-Worth in Action

To live your self-worth, start incorporating intentional choices into your daily routine. Here are a few examples:

- How You Speak to Yourself
  - Instead of criticizing yourself for a mistake, try saying, *"It's okay to make mistakes. I'm learning and growing."*
  - Replace self-doubt with affirmations like, *"I am capable and deserving of success."*
- How You Spend Your Time
  - Prioritize activities that bring you joy, peace, or growth.
  - Say no to commitments that don't align with your values or drain your energy.
- How You Allow Others to Treat You
  - Set boundaries with people who disrespect your time or emotions.
  - Surround yourself with those who celebrate your worth and encourage your growth.

- How You Care for Your Body and Mind
    - Take time for physical activity, nourishing meals, and rest.
    - Engage in practices that calm your mind, like meditation or journaling.

Creating an Environment That Reflects Your Worth

Your surroundings have a powerful impact on how you feel and act. A cluttered, chaotic space can make you feel overwhelmed, while a clean, calming environment can inspire peace and focus. Living self-worth means creating an environment that supports and reflects your values.

Practical Tips

- Declutter: Remove items that no longer serve you. Let go of things that carry negative memories or emotions.
- Add Joyful Touches: Surround yourself with things that bring you joy, a favorite book, a scented candle, or fresh flowers.
- Set Boundaries with Your Space: Create areas dedicated to rest, work, or creativity, and use them intentionally.

A Daily Practice, Not Perfection

Living your self-worth doesn't mean getting it right all the time. There will be days when you make choices that don't fully align with your value, and that's okay. What matters is the intention to keep trying, to keep choosing yourself, even when it's hard.

Reflection Prompt

- Ask yourself: *What's one small choice I can make today to honor my worth?*

Living self-worth is about transforming belief into action, one choice at a time. In the next section, we'll explore how setting boundaries is a powerful act of self-respect and a vital part of living your self-worth.

The Role of Boundaries

Living your self-worth is not just about recognizing your value; it's about protecting it. Boundaries are the invisible lines you draw to safeguard your time, energy, and emotional well-being. They aren't selfish or mean, they're necessary acts of self-respect that honor your worth and define how you want to engage with the world around you.

But here's the truth: setting boundaries can feel uncomfortable, especially if you're someone who's used to putting others' needs above your own. Society often praises selflessness, leaving many of us to feel guilty for saying no or prioritizing ourselves. Yet boundaries are the foundation for healthy relationships, with others and with yourself. Without them, you risk exhaustion, resentment, and a diminished sense of self.

Why Boundaries Are a Form of Self-Worth

When you set a boundary, you're sending a powerful message to yourself: *"I matter. My needs matter. My well-being matters."* This act of self-respect reinforces your worth, not just in your own eyes but also in the eyes of those around you.

Think of boundaries as a way of teaching others how to treat you. Without clear boundaries, people may unknowingly overstep, leaving you feeling unheard or undervalued. But with boundaries, you set the standard for how you want to be treated.

The Emotional Benefits of Boundaries

Establishing boundaries doesn't just protect your time and energy, it also nurtures your emotional health. Here's how:

- Prevents Burnout: By saying no to unnecessary demands, you reserve energy for what truly matters.

- Reduces Resentment: Boundaries eliminate the frustration that comes from feeling taken advantage of.

- Builds Confidence: Each time you uphold a boundary, you reinforce the belief that you are deserving of respect.

"When we fail to set boundaries and hold people accountable, we feel used and mistreated." – Brené Brown

Boundaries Are Not Barriers

One common misconception is that boundaries are walls meant to shut people out. In reality, boundaries are bridges that allow you to connect with others in healthier and more meaningful ways. They create clarity and mutual understanding, ensuring that both your needs and the needs of others are respected.

Imagine trying to navigate a relationship without boundaries. You might find yourself overextending, constantly guessing what's acceptable, or feeling hurt when someone unintentionally crosses a line. Boundaries remove the guesswork. They make your expectations clear, giving others the opportunity to meet them.

Signs You Need Stronger Boundaries

Boundaries often become necessary when you notice patterns of discomfort or imbalance in your life. These signs can serve as red flags that it's time to make a change:

- Chronic Exhaustion: If you constantly feel drained, it may be because you're giving too much of your energy without replenishing it.

- Frequent Resentment: Feeling annoyed or bitter after helping someone is often a sign that you've overstepped your own limits.

- Difficulty Saying No: If you find yourself saying yes to things you'd rather avoid, you may need to practice asserting your boundaries.

- Feeling Taken for Granted: When others assume you'll always say yes or be available, it's a sign that your boundaries aren't clear.

Why Boundaries Feel Difficult

If setting boundaries feels hard, you're not alone. Many of us were taught to prioritize others' feelings over our own. Perhaps you grew up believing that saying no was rude or selfish, or maybe you fear conflict and avoid setting boundaries to keep the peace. These fears are valid but must be challenged.

Common Fears About Boundaries

- Fear of Rejection: Worrying that setting a boundary will push people away.
- Fear of Guilt: Feeling selfish for putting your needs first.
- Fear of Conflict: Avoiding boundaries to prevent arguments or hurt feelings.

While these fears may hold you back initially, it's important to remember that boundaries are acts of love, not just for yourself, but for others too. They allow you to show up authentically and ensure that your relationships are rooted in mutual respect.

Reframing the Fear

Instead of thinking, *"What if they get upset?"* ask yourself, *"What if I continue to neglect my needs?"* The cost of not setting boundaries is often far greater than the temporary discomfort of establishing them.

Practical Steps to Set Boundaries

Setting boundaries can feel intimidating at first, especially if you're used to putting others' needs before your own. But with practice, it becomes easier and more natural.

1. Reflect on Your Needs

- *Ask yourself: What do I need to feel respected and supported in this situation?*
- *Identify specific behaviors or circumstances that cross your boundaries.*

2. Communicate Clearly

- Use direct, respectful language to express your boundaries.

  - Example: *"I need uninterrupted time to focus on my work. Please knock before entering my office."*

- Avoid over-explaining or apologizing for your needs.

3. Stay Consistent

- Enforce your boundaries firmly but kindly. Consistency teaches others to respect your limits.

- If someone repeatedly ignores your boundaries, reevaluate the relationship and consider whether adjustments are needed.

4. Practice Saying No

- Saying no is a complete sentence and an essential part of setting boundaries.

- Example: *"Thank you for thinking of me, but I'm not available for that right now."*

Navigating Pushback

It's natural to face resistance when you first start setting boundaries, especially if others are used to you always saying yes. Remember, pushback is a reflection of their discomfort, not a sign that your boundary is wrong.

How to Handle Pushback

- Stay Calm: Respond with patience and firmness.

- Reiterate Your Boundary: *"I understand this might feel new, but this is what I need to take care of myself."*

- Let Go of Guilt: Setting boundaries isn't selfish, it's self-care.

Boundaries and Your Self-Worth

Every time you set and uphold a boundary, you're affirming your worth. You're saying, *"My needs matter, and I deserve to be treated with respect."* Over time, this practice strengthens your self-esteem and creates healthier, more balanced relationships.

Reflection Prompt

- Think of a situation where you felt disrespected or overextended. What boundary could you set to protect yourself in the future?

In the next section, we'll dive into nurturing your mind, body, and spirit as a reflection of self-worth. Living your worth isn't just about boundaries, it's also about how you care for your whole self.

Nurturing Your Mind, Body, and Spirit

Living your self-worth isn't just about setting boundaries or making intentional choices, it's also about caring for the whole person you are: your mind, body, and spirit. Self-care isn't a luxury or an indulgence; it's a fundamental way to affirm your value and show yourself the love and respect you deserve.

When you nurture your well-being, you're not just taking care of your physical health, you're also cultivating emotional resilience, mental clarity, and spiritual alignment. This holistic approach creates a strong foundation for living your self-worth every day.

Why Holistic Care Matters

Your mind, body, and spirit are deeply interconnected. Neglecting one aspect of your well-being often affects the others. For instance, stress from neglecting your mental health can lead to physical exhaustion, while a lack of spiritual grounding can make it harder to find peace in challenging times. Caring for yourself holistically ensures that all parts of you are supported and aligned.

"Take care of your body. It's the only place you have to live." – Jim Rohn

Caring for Your Mind

Your mind is where your thoughts, beliefs, and perceptions are shaped, and these have a direct impact on your sense of self-worth. To live your worth, it's essential to cultivate a healthy, nurturing mental environment.

Practical Ways to Nurture Your Mind

- Practice Gratitude
  - Start or end each day by listing three things you're grateful for.
  - Gratitude helps shift your focus from what's lacking to what's abundant in your life.
- Challenge Negative Thoughts
  - When self-doubt arises, ask yourself: Is this thought based on fact, or is it fear speaking?
  - Replace critical thoughts with affirming ones, such as: "I am doing the best I can, and that is enough."
- Engage in Lifelong Learning

- Feed your mind with knowledge that excites and empowers you, whether through books, podcasts, or courses.
- Prioritize Mental Breaks
  - Allow yourself moments of stillness to recharge, whether through meditation, a walk in nature, or quiet reflection.

Caring for Your Body

Your body is your home, the vessel that carries you through life. Living your self-worth means treating your body with kindness, respect, and care. This isn't about striving for perfection, it's about honoring the incredible things your body does for you every day.

Practical Ways to Nurture Your Body

- Move with Intention
  - Find physical activities that bring you joy, whether it's dancing, yoga, weightlifting, or simply taking a walk.
- Nourish Yourself
  - Choose foods that energize and sustain you, focusing on balance rather than restriction.
  - Hydrate regularly, it's a simple but powerful act of self-care.
- Rest Without Guilt
  - Listen to your body's signals and allow yourself to rest when you're tired. Rest is productive and essential.
- Celebrate Your Body
  - Instead of focusing on flaws, appreciate your body for what it allows you to do.

- For example, thank your legs for carrying you, your hands for creating, or your heart for beating tirelessly.

Caring for Your Spirit

Your spirit is the essence of who you are, the part of you that seeks meaning, connection, and peace. When you nurture your spirit, you align with your values and purpose, creating a sense of harmony and fulfillment.

Practical Ways to Nurture Your Spirit

- Connect with Something Greater
  - This might mean prayer, meditation, or spending time in nature. Find what makes you feel connected to the world around you.
- Engage in Practices That Uplift You
  - Whether it's journaling, creating art, or listening to inspiring music, prioritize activities that feed your soul.
- Cultivate a Sense of Purpose
  - Reflect on what gives your life meaning. How can you align your daily actions with your deeper values?
- Foster Relationships That Inspire You
  - Surround yourself with people who encourage your growth and share your vision for a fulfilling life.

Reflection Prompt

As you reflect on the ways you care for your mind, body, and spirit, ask yourself:

- *Where am I thriving, and where might I need more support?*

- *What small change can I make today to better nurture myself holistically?*

In the next section, we'll explore how to build a life that aligns with your values, creating a daily reality that reflects your worth and priorities. Living self-worth isn't just about care, it's about intention and alignment.

Building a Life Aligned with Your Values

Living your self-worth isn't just about knowing your values, it's about embedding them into the fabric of your daily life. This section will be a practical guide, helping you take meaningful steps to align your habits, routines, and decisions with the principles that matter most to you. It's not about achieving perfection overnight; it's about building a life that reflects your worth, one intentional choice at a time.

When your actions align with your values, you create a life that feels authentic and fulfilling. This alignment ensures that your time, energy, and focus are directed toward what truly matters, giving you a deeper sense of purpose and peace.

Why Alignment Matters

When your life aligns with your values, everything begins to flow. You're no longer fighting against the tide of others' expectations or settling for what doesn't feel right. Instead, you're living in harmony with your truth, which creates a sense of peace, clarity, and purpose.

The Impact of Misalignment

- Emotional Disconnect: You may feel unfulfilled or restless without knowing why.

- Increased Stress: Living against your values often leads to burnout or frustration.

- Loss of Identity: Over time, compromising your values can make you feel disconnected from who you are.

Aligning your life with your values allows you to live intentionally, not reactively. It's a way of saying, *"This is who I am, and I will honor that in everything I do."*

How to Identify Your Core Values

Your core values are the guiding principles that shape your decisions and define what's truly important to you. They are the foundation of a meaningful, fulfilling life.

Steps to Identify Your Core Values

- Reflect on What Matters Most
    - Ask yourself: What brings me joy? What gives me a sense of purpose?
    - Consider moments when you felt truly alive or fulfilled, what values were at play?
- Examine Your Role Models
    - Think about people you admire. What qualities or principles do they embody?
    - These traits often reveal your own values.
- List and Prioritize

- Write down a list of potential values (e.g., honesty, creativity, family, health, freedom).
- Narrow it down to the top 3–5 that resonate most deeply with you.

Reflection Prompt

- *What values have guided my best decisions? How can I make them more present in my daily life?*

Creating Habits That Reflect Your Values

Once you've identified your core values, the next step is to align your habits and routines with them. This process ensures that your daily life supports the person you want to be.

Practical Strategies

- Audit Your Time
  - Track how you spend your time for a week.
  - Compare this to your values. Are your actions reflecting what matters most to you?
- Set Value-Driven Goals
  - For each core value, create a specific, actionable goal.
  - Example: If *health* is a value, commit to a 20-minute daily walk or meal prepping each week.
- Simplify Your Commitments
  - Eliminate activities or obligations that don't align with your values.
  - Practice saying no to things that don't serve your goals or priorities.

- Celebrate Progress
  - Recognize and reward yourself for making choices that honor your values.

Example: A Day Aligned with Your Values

- Morning: Meditate for 10 minutes to nurture your spiritual connection.
- Afternoon: Dedicate focused time to a work project that aligns with your purpose.
- Evening: Cook a healthy dinner and spend quality time with loved ones.

Living Your Values in Relationships

Your relationships are one of the most significant areas where your values come to life. Living self-worth means fostering connections that reflect your principles and bring out the best in you.

How to Align Relationships with Your Values

- Communicate Clearly: Share your values with those close to you. Let them know what's important to you and why.
- Set Boundaries: Uphold boundaries that protect your values, such as prioritizing family time or saying no to toxic dynamics.
- Seek Reciprocity: Surround yourself with people who respect and support your values, and offer the same in return.

Reflection Prompt

- Ask yourself: *Do my relationships reflect and honor my values? If not, what changes can I make?*

The Long-Term Benefits of Alignment

When you build a life that aligns with your values, you:

- Experience a greater sense of purpose and direction.
- Cultivate deeper, more meaningful relationships.
- Feel more confident and at peace with your choices.

Alignment isn't about perfection, it's about progress. Each intentional choice brings you closer to a life that truly reflects your worth and priorities.

In the next section, we'll explore how to overcome challenges like self-doubt, guilt, and fear that often arise when living your self-worth. These obstacles don't have to hold you back, they can become opportunities for growth.

Overcoming Challenges to Living Self-Worth

Living your self-worth is a powerful declaration to yourself and the world: *I am valuable, deserving, and enough.* But this choice, as transformative as it is, comes with challenges. Along the way, you'll encounter inner struggles like self-doubt, guilt, or fear of judgment, and external resistance from people who may not understand or support your growth.

Here's the truth: these challenges are not a sign of failure, they're proof that you're growing. Growth, by its very nature, pushes you beyond your comfort zone and into new, unfamiliar territory. It asks you to shed old beliefs and habits that no longer serve you. And yes, it can feel uncomfortable, even painful at times. But every time you confront these obstacles, you strengthen your resolve, deepen your sense of self-worth, and move closer to the life you deserve.

The Challenges Are Part of the Journey

Imagine planting a seed. At first, the seed is buried in darkness, surrounded by soil. For it to grow, it must push through the dirt, break the surface, and stretch toward the sun. The seed doesn't grow despite the challenges, it grows because of them.

In the same way, the challenges you face as you live your self-worth are not roadblocks but stepping stones. They teach you resilience, strengthen your boundaries, and clarify your values. Each obstacle is an opportunity to reaffirm your worth and demonstrate, to yourself and others, that you are committed to honoring it.

Reflection Prompt

- *Ask yourself: What if these challenges aren't here to stop me, but to strengthen me?* What if they are proof of my growth?

Why Challenges Often Arise

Challenges often arise because living your self-worth means rewriting old patterns. You're breaking free from limiting beliefs, redefining relationships, and prioritizing yourself in ways you may not have before. This shift can feel disruptive, both to you and those around you.

Common Reasons for Challenges

- Internal Resistance: Your mind may cling to old habits or fears, questioning whether you're truly worthy.

- External Pushback: People who are used to the "old you" might struggle to accept the changes you're making.

- Fear of the Unknown: Change can feel uncertain and unsettling, even when it's positive.

Acknowledging these challenges as natural and expected can help you face them with compassion and courage.

Reframing Challenges as Opportunities

Every challenge carries a lesson, and every lesson is a chance to grow. When you reframe obstacles as opportunities, you shift from feeling defeated to feeling empowered.

- **Self-Doubt Becomes Self-Discovery**: Instead of seeing self-doubt as a weakness, view it as an invitation to uncover and challenge limiting beliefs.

- **Guilt Becomes Self-Acceptance**: Let guilt remind you of your worth, as you learn to prioritize yourself without shame.

- **Fear Becomes Courage**: Fear signals that you're stepping into something new and meaningful.

"Out of difficulties grow miracles." – Jean de La Bruyère

Each time you navigate a challenge, you create your own small miracle, proof that you're capable of choosing yourself, even when it's hard.

The Transformative Power of Persistence

Living your self-worth is not a one-time decision; it's a practice. And like any practice, it requires persistence. There will be days when the old doubts creep in, when others question your choices, or when it feels easier to revert to old habits. But those are the moments that matter most.

Every time you choose to keep going, you reinforce the belief that you are worthy of the effort. Over time, this persistence becomes your strength. It becomes the foundation on which you build a life that reflects your true value.

Reflection Prompt

- Think about a time when you overcame a challenge and felt stronger on the other side. How did that experience shape your view of yourself?

Encouragement for the Journey

Living your self-worth isn't a straight path. It's a winding journey with highs and lows, victories and setbacks. But with every step, you're learning, growing, and becoming more aligned with the person you were always meant to be.

As you face challenges, remember:

- **You are not alone**: Others have walked this path and emerged stronger.
- **You are capable**: Every challenge is an opportunity to prove your strength.
- **You are worthy**: Your worth doesn't depend on your circumstances or others' opinions, it simply is.

Let each obstacle you encounter be a reminder of your courage and a step closer to the life you deserve.

Practical Tools to Navigate Challenges

Facing challenges to living your self-worth can feel overwhelming, but with the right tools, you can overcome them with grace and strength. These strategies are designed to help you navigate self-doubt, guilt, fear of judgment, and resistance while staying firmly rooted in your values.

1. Journaling: Your Safe Space for Reflection

Journaling is a powerful way to process emotions, gain clarity, and track your growth. It provides a non-judgmental space where you can explore your thoughts and feelings, uncover limiting beliefs, and identify patterns that no longer serve you.

How to Use Journaling

- Process Self-Doubt: Write about a moment when self-doubt crept in. Reflect on where it came from and what evidence supports or contradicts it.

- Reframe Guilt: If you feel guilty about prioritizing yourself, journal about why you deserve care and how honoring your needs benefits others, too.

- Set Intentions: Begin each day by writing one small way you will honor your worth.

Prompt to Try

- *What challenge am I currently facing, and what lesson might it be teaching me?*

2. Affirmations: Rewiring Your Inner Dialogue

Affirmations help counteract negative self-talk and reinforce positive beliefs. When repeated consistently, they can rewire your brain to think more compassionately and confidently.

Examples of Affirmations

- *"I am worthy of love, respect, and care."*
- *"I have the strength to overcome challenges and grow from them."*
- *"My worth is not determined by others' opinions."*

How to Incorporate Affirmations

- Write them on sticky notes and place them where you'll see them daily, on your mirror, desk, or phone.
- Say them aloud in the morning or before bed to set a positive tone for your day.
- Pair affirmations with deep breaths to calm your nervous system and enhance their impact.

3. Grounding Techniques: Finding Stability in Emotional Storms

When challenges feel overwhelming, grounding exercises can bring you back to the present moment, helping you manage anxiety and refocus your energy.

Simple Grounding Exercises

- **5-4-3-2-1 Technique**: Identify 5 things you can see, 4 things you can touch, 3 things you can hear, 2 things you can smell, and 1 thing you can taste.

- **Deep Breathing**: Breathe in for a count of 4, hold for 4, and exhale for 4. Repeat until you feel calmer.

- **Body Scan**: Close your eyes and focus on each part of your body, starting at your toes and working upward, releasing tension as you go.

4. Building a Support System

You don't have to face challenges alone. Surrounding yourself with supportive, like-minded people can make all the difference in staying committed to your self-worth.

Ways to Build Support

- Confide in Trusted Friends or Family: Share your journey and let them know how they can support you.

- Join a Community: Find groups or forums where others are on similar paths of self-discovery and growth.

- Work with a Coach or Therapist: Professionals can provide valuable tools, insights, and encouragement to navigate obstacles.

Reflection Prompt

- *Who in my life can I turn to for support, and how can I nurture that connection?*

5. Reframing Challenges as Growth Opportunities

Challenges often feel like setbacks, but with practice, you can learn to see them as opportunities for growth. This shift in perspective can empower you to face obstacles with resilience and hope.

How to Reframe Challenges

- *Ask Empowering Questions: Instead of asking, "Why is this happening to me?" ask, "What can I learn from this?"*

- **Celebrate Small Wins**: Acknowledge every step forward, even if it's just recognizing your effort to keep going.

- **Visualize Your Progress**: Picture yourself a year from now, stronger and more confident because you overcame this challenge.

6. Setting Boundaries to Protect Your Growth

As you face challenges, it's crucial to create space for your growth by setting boundaries. This includes protecting your time, energy, and emotional well-being from distractions or negativity.

Practical Boundary-Setting Tips

- Prioritize Yourself: Block out time in your schedule for self-care, reflection, or rest.

- Say No Without Guilt: Remember, every time you say no to something misaligned with your worth, you're saying yes to yourself.

- Limit Toxic Influences: Reduce interactions with people or situations that undermine your confidence or self-worth.

7. Practicing Self-Compassion

When you face setbacks or feel challenged, self-compassion is your greatest ally. It reminds you to treat yourself with the same kindness and understanding you'd offer a close friend.

Ways to Practice Self-Compassion

- **Speak Kindly to Yourself**: Replace harsh self-criticism with affirming statements like, *"It's okay to feel this way. I'm doing the best I can."*

- **Give Yourself Permission to Rest**: Recognize that rest and recovery are essential parts of growth.

- **Acknowledge Your Efforts**: Celebrate the fact that you're trying, even when it feels difficult.

Challenges are inevitable, but so is your ability to overcome them. You have the tools, the strength, and the courage to navigate anything that comes your way. Remember, every step you take to face these obstacles reaffirms your worth and brings you closer to the life you deserve.

"The strongest oak of the forest is not the one that is protected from the storm, but the one that stands in the open where it is compelled to struggle for its existence against the winds and rains and the scorching sun." – Napoleon Hill

Embrace the storms as part of your journey. They are shaping you into the person you were always meant to be.

In the next section, we'll provide practical exercises to help you strengthen your commitment to living your self-worth every day. These exercises are designed to empower you to navigate challenges and embody your value with confidence and resilience

Daily Practices to Embody Self-Worth

Putting self-worth into practice is the key to transforming it from a concept into a lived reality. These exercises are designed to help you integrate self-worth into your daily life, strengthen your confidence, and navigate challenges with grace. Each activity offers an opportunity to affirm your value and build habits that reflect your worth.

1. The "Worthiness Audit"

Purpose

To evaluate areas of your life where your actions align with your self-worth, and where they don't, so you can make intentional adjustments.

Steps

- Divide a Page into Two Columns
  - On the left, write "Aligned with My Worth."
  - On the right, write "Misaligned with My Worth."
- Reflect on Key Areas of Your Life
  - Relationships, work, self-care, and personal boundaries.
- Evaluate Actions
  - For each area, write down behaviors, habits, or situations that either affirm or diminish your self-worth.
- Identify Small Changes
  - Choose one action from the "Misaligned" column to address this week.

Example

- Aligned with My Worth: Saying no to an extra work project when I needed rest.
- Misaligned with My Worth: Letting a friend repeatedly cancel plans without addressing it.

2. Daily Affirmation Ritual

Purpose

To rewire your inner dialogue and replace self-doubt with empowering beliefs.

Steps

- Choose 1–3 affirmations that resonate with you (e.g., *"I am worthy of respect and love."*).
- Repeat them aloud in the morning, while looking in the mirror, to set a positive tone for your day.
- Write them in a journal before bed to reinforce them.

Advanced Tip

Pair affirmations with a physical gesture, like placing your hand on your heart, to deepen the connection.

3. The "Boundary Map"

Purpose

To identify and establish boundaries that protect your time, energy, and well-being.

Steps

- List Common Scenarios

- Identify situations where you feel drained, resentful, or overextended (e.g., agreeing to tasks you don't have time for).
- Define Your Limits
  - For each scenario, write down what you're no longer willing to tolerate and how you'll communicate your boundary.
- Practice Saying No
  - Use clear, respectful phrases like: *"I appreciate you thinking of me, but I can't take that on right now."*

4. Self-Care Menu

Purpose

To create a personalized list of self-care activities that nurture your mind, body, and spirit.

Steps

- Divide a page into three sections: Mind, Body, Spirit.
- Under each section, list activities that make you feel cared for and recharged.
- Commit to one activity from each section every week.

Examples

- Mind: Journaling, reading a book, learning something new.
- Body: Stretching, walking, eating nourishing meals.
- Spirit: Meditation, prayer, spending time in nature.

5. Visualization Practice: Living Your Self-Worth

Purpose

To connect with your future self and gain clarity on how living self-worth transforms your life.

Steps

- Find a quiet place where you won't be disturbed. Close your eyes and take a few deep breaths.
- Imagine yourself one year from now, living fully aligned with your self-worth.
  - What does your day look like?
  - How do you feel?
  - Who are you surrounded by?
- Write down what you envisioned and one action you can take today to move closer to that life.

"Create the highest, grandest vision possible for your life, because you become what you believe." – Oprah Winfrey

6. Gratitude Check-In

Purpose

To shift your focus from what's missing to what's abundant in your life, reinforcing a mindset of self-worth.

Steps

- Set aside five minutes each evening.
- Write down three things you're grateful for that day.

- Reflect on how these moments align with your values and worth.

Example

- *Grateful for: Setting a boundary with a coworker. Feeling appreciated by a loved one. Taking a peaceful walk after work.*

7. "Self-Worth Compass" Worksheet

Purpose

To guide your decisions based on your values and worth.

Steps

- When faced with a decision, ask yourself:
  - Does this align with my values?
  - Does this honor my worth?
  - Will this decision bring me closer to the life I want?
- Write down your answers in the worksheet to clarify your intentions.

These exercises are not meant to be overwhelming, they're tools to help you take small, intentional steps toward living your self-worth. Choose one or two practices that resonate with you and integrate them into your routine. Over time, these small actions will create big shifts, reinforcing your value in every area of your life.

"What you practice, you become. Let self-worth be the practice that transforms your life." – Unknown

Your Self-Worth, Your Legacy

Living your self-worth is not just a journey, it's a declaration, a practice, and ultimately, a legacy. It's the ripple effect of choosing yourself, every single day, that extends beyond your own life and touches the lives of those around you.

As you've moved through this book, you've explored what it means to embrace self-worth, set boundaries, align with your values, and overcome challenges. Each chapter has been a step toward recognizing that you are deserving, not because of what you do or achieve, but because of who you are.

The Gift of Living Authentically

When you live your self-worth, you give yourself permission to show up authentically in the world. This authenticity is magnetic, it inspires others to do the same. Your choice to live aligned with your worth becomes a model for your loved ones, your community, and even strangers who witness your light.

Reflection Prompt

- *Ask yourself: What kind of legacy do I want to leave behind? How can living my self-worth shape that legacy?*

The Courage to Keep Choosing Yourself

This journey isn't linear, and it isn't without its challenges. There will be days when self-doubt resurfaces, when others resist your growth, or when old habits call you back. But each day also brings new opportunities to reaffirm your value, to realign with your vision, and to take one more step toward the life you deserve.

"The most courageous act is still to think for yourself. Aloud." – Coco Chanel

Every choice to honor your worth is an act of courage, and every act of courage reinforces the truth: *You are enough.*

When you live your self-worth, you not only transform your own life but also create a ripple effect that impacts others. Your confidence, boundaries, and values inspire those around you to reflect on their own lives. Imagine a world where more people understood their worth, where compassion, respect, and empowerment became the norm. Your journey is part of that greater vision.

Your Legacy in Action

- **In Relationships**: By honoring your worth, you teach others to respect and value themselves.

- **In Your Work**: Your alignment with your values brings purpose and authenticity to your contributions.

- **In Your Community**: Your courage to live authentically inspires others to do the same.

This book is just the beginning. The real transformation happens in the daily practice of living your self-worth. It's in the moments when you choose to say no to what doesn't serve you, yes to what aligns with your values, and compassion to yourself when the journey feels hard.

Remember, your worth is not something you have to earn, it's already within you. All that's left is to live it, boldly and unapologetically.

As you close this book, take a moment to reflect on what resonated most with you. What one action can you take today to honor your worth? Write it down, commit to it, and take that first step.

Reflection Prompt

- *How will I honor my self-worth today, tomorrow, and in the months ahead?*

Outro: Becoming the Architect of Your New Identity

1. Embracing the Journey of Becoming

You've come so far. Pause for a moment and let that sink in. The person who started reading this book, the one who was questioning their worth, doubting their strength, and wondering if change was possible, is not the same person who stands here now. You've grown. You've faced truths that were hard to confront. You've taken steps that required courage. And now, you're stepping into something extraordinary: the beginning of a life that reflects your true, beautiful, undeniable worth.

This is more than the end of a book. It's the start of a new chapter in your life, a chapter where you get to take everything you've learned and use it to design a future that honors who you are. It won't always be easy, but I need you to hear this: *You are capable. You are worthy. And you are not alone.*

"The moment you doubt whether you can fly, you cease forever to be able to do it." – J.M. Barrie, Peter Pan

2. The Power of Living Authentically

Living your self-worth means showing up in the world as your full, authentic self. It means no longer shrinking to fit into others' expectations or apologizing for who you are. It's stepping into your truth, owning your value, and creating a life that reflects your deepest desires and values.

But authenticity is more than a personal triumph, it's a gift to the world. When you live authentically, you become a source of light and inspiration. You show others what it means to live with courage and purpose. You remind them that they, too, can honor their worth.

Reflection Prompt

- *Who am I becoming as I embrace my authentic self, and how might my journey inspire those around me?*

You may feel vulnerable as you step into this new way of being. That's natural. Authenticity takes bravery, but every time you choose it, you build a life that feels true and meaningful. And you are never alone in this. There are others, like me, cheering you on every step of the way.

3. Reframing Setbacks as Growth Opportunities

Let's be honest: the road ahead won't be without its bumps. There will be days when you question your progress, when old patterns try to pull you back, or when others don't understand your growth. These moments can feel discouraging, but they are not the end. They are simply part of the process.

Every setback you face is an opportunity to learn, grow, and reaffirm your worth. Instead of seeing challenges as roadblocks, see them as stepping stones. Each one teaches you something about your strength, your values, and your ability to persevere.

"The oak fought the wind and was broken, the willow bent when it must and survived." – Robert Jordan

On the hard days, remember that setbacks don't erase your progress. They don't define you. What defines you is the way you rise, the way you keep going, and the way you remind yourself that *you are worthy, even in the struggle.*

4. Building a Legacy of Self-Worth

Your journey doesn't stop with you. By living your self-worth, you're creating a ripple effect that touches everyone around you. Your courage to honor your value shows others that they can do the same. Your authenticity inspires your friends, your family, and even strangers who cross your path.

Think about the legacy you're building. What message do you want to leave behind for those you love? For future generations? Living your self-worth isn't just about creating a life you love, it's about showing others what's possible when you choose to embrace your inherent value.

Reflection Prompt

- *What impact do I want my journey of self-worth to have on the people around me?*

You have the power to change not only your life but also the lives of those who look up to you. Your legacy will be one of courage, love, and unwavering belief in the value of every person, starting with yourself.

5. Action Steps for Continuing the Journey

Here's how to keep building on the foundation you've created:

- **Daily Affirmations**: Start each day with a statement of your worth (e.g., *"I am deserving of love, success, and peace."*).

- **Reflection Time**: Dedicate a few minutes each week to assess how you're living in alignment with your values.

- **Set One Bold Goal**: Choose one dream that feels exciting and a little scary, and commit to taking small steps toward it.

- **Celebrate Progress**: Keep a journal of your wins, no matter how small, to remind yourself of your growth.

- **Connect with a Support System**: Surround yourself with people who uplift you and hold you accountable to your worth.

6. Closing Reflection: The Future You Are Creating

Take a deep breath. Close your eyes. Picture the person you are becoming. She is confident. She is courageous. She is living a life that honors her worth. This person is *you.*

The future you are creating isn't a distant dream, it's unfolding with every choice you make, every boundary you set, and every moment you choose to honor yourself.

"Go confidently in the direction of your dreams. Live the life you have imagined." – Henry David Thoreau

Step into this future boldly, knowing that you are the architect of a life that is uniquely, beautifully, and powerfully yours.

A Message from Sabrina

Dear Reader,

As you close this book, I want you to know how proud I am of you. Whether you completed every exercise, read the chapters slowly, or skipped around to what resonated most, you've shown courage and commitment to yourself. And that's no small thing.

Choosing to embark on a journey of self-worth is one of the bravest decisions you can make. It's a choice to believe in your inherent value, even when the world tries to tell you otherwise. It's a choice to stand up for yourself, to honor your needs, and to build a life that reflects the amazing person you are.

I've walked this path too. I know the doubt, the fear, and the weight of wondering if things can truly change. But I also know the beauty of what lies on the other side. I've seen it in my own life, in the lives of my clients, and now, in yours.

The journey to self-worth isn't always linear. There will be days when you feel unstoppable, and others when old habits or doubts creep back in. That's okay. Growth isn't about being perfect, it's about showing up for yourself, again and again.

You've already proven you can do that. You've taken the time to reflect, to heal, and to begin creating the life you deserve. That's something to celebrate. You are more capable and resilient than you realize, and the steps you've taken here are just the beginning of what you're capable of achieving.

I want you to remember this: you are never alone on this journey. Every challenge you face, every victory you celebrate, every quiet moment of reflection, you are supported. By this book, by the tools you've gained, and by the hope that brought you here in the first place.

And though I may not know you personally, I am rooting for you. I am cheering for the person you are becoming, for the courage it takes to choose self-worth, and for the light you will bring into this world by living authentically.

As you turn the final page of this book, take a deep breath and hold onto this truth: You are enough, just as you are. Your worth isn't something you have to earn, it's already within you. Every step you take from here is an act of honoring that worth and building a life that reflects it.

The road ahead may have its challenges, but you are equipped to navigate them. Remember the tools you've gained, the strength you've discovered, and the vision you've created. You have everything you need to move forward with confidence and purpose.

Thank you for allowing me to be a part of your journey. Writing this book was a labor of love, and my greatest hope is that it has offered you even a fraction of the inspiration and empowerment you've brought into your own life by reading it.

I believe in you. I see your strength, your courage, and your worth. And I know that the life you are building will be as extraordinary as the person creating it.

Go forward boldly. Trust yourself. And remember: you are worthy, always.

With all my love and encouragement,

Sabrina

(Your fellow traveler on this journey of self-worth)

"You may not control all the events that happen to you, but you can decide not to be reduced by them." – Maya Angelou

Voices of Transformation: Stories of Healing and Empowerment from Sabrina's Clients

Throughout this journey, you've been encouraged to embrace your self-worth, overcome challenges, and live authentically. Now, let's hear from others who have walked a similar path. These powerful stories of transformation highlight the real-life impact of choosing self-worth and the profound guidance Sabrina has provided as a coach and mentor. Each testimonial is a testament to the resilience, courage, and beauty that emerge when one decides to heal and grow.

Testimonial 1: Breaking Free from Self-Doubt

"If you get the chance to work with Sabrina, take it. I had the privilege of spending 12 weeks with her as my coach, and I can honestly say it changed my life. Sabrina has this incredible intuition, she knows where your struggles are, even when you're not sure yourself. She helped me confront my self-doubt head-on, gently but firmly guiding me toward clarity and confidence."

This client, like so many others, found herself trapped in the grip of self-doubt. For years, she questioned her abilities, second-guessed her decisions, and held back from pursuing her dreams. Working with Sabrina was her turning point.

Through personalized coaching and exercises that focused on reframing negative self-talk and identifying her unique strengths, she began to see herself in a new light. Step by step, she replaced her inner critic with a voice of compassion and confidence. Today, she describes herself as a woman who "stands tall, knows her worth, and isn't afraid to own it."

Reflection for the Reader

- Have you ever felt held back by self-doubt? How might you take a step toward freeing yourself from it today?

Testimonial 2: Redefining Self-Worth with Sabrina's Guidance

"I've worked with other therapists, but Sabrina is truly something special. She has this God-given ability to see your heart, even when it feels buried under layers of pain and fear. She taught me how to redefine my self-worth, not based on what others thought of me, but on who I truly am."

For this client, the journey of self-worth began in a place of brokenness. Years of people-pleasing and sacrificing her own needs had left her feeling invisible and unfulfilled. Sabrina's approach was both empathetic and empowering, helping her to see that her value wasn't tied to her roles or responsibilities but was inherent and unshakable.

Together, they worked on boundary-setting, daily affirmations, and practical tools to nurture self-love. The result? A profound transformation. She now describes her life as "aligned with my values and filled with relationships that reflect my worth."

Reflection for the Reader

- What would it mean for you to redefine your self-worth? How might that shift change your relationships and choices?

Testimonial 3: Embracing Growth and Forgiveness

"Sabrina's coaching didn't just change my mindset, it changed my life. She helped me process years of pain and trauma, guiding me to a place of growth and forgiveness. Her ability to create a safe, supportive space made all the difference. With her help, I found the strength to let go of the past and embrace the future with hope."

This client's journey was one of deep healing. Haunted by past mistakes and unresolved pain, she felt stuck in a cycle of self-blame and regret. Sabrina's guidance provided the tools to break free, starting with radical self-compassion.

Through reflective exercises and heartfelt conversations, she learned to release guilt, forgive herself, and focus on the possibilities ahead. Today, she views her past not as a burden but as a foundation for growth, and she's actively building a life that reflects her newfound freedom.

Reflection for the Reader

- Is there something in your past that you need to forgive yourself for? How might forgiveness open the door to growth?

These stories are a reminder that transformation is possible for anyone willing to take the first step. Whether you're struggling with self-doubt, redefining your worth, or seeking healing and forgiveness, know that you are not alone. The journey isn't always easy, but as these testimonials show, it's always worth it.

Appendices

Appendix A: Extended Exercises and Templates

Self-Worth Action Plan Worksheet

This worksheet is designed to help you map out a personalized plan for living your self-worth daily. Use it as a practical tool to set goals, track progress, and reflect on your journey.

- **Vision for Self-Worth**
    - What does living your self-worth look like?
    - Write down three to five specific ways you want to embody your worth in your daily life.
- **Daily Affirmations**
    - List three affirmations you will repeat each morning to reinforce your value.
- **Weekly Reflection**
    - At the end of each week, answer:
        - How did I honor my worth this week?
        - What challenges did I face, and how did I navigate them?
        - What is one thing I will do differently next week?
- **Monthly Check-In**
    - Revisit your vision for self-worth.
    - Adjust your goals and practices as needed.

Boundary-Setting Guide

Setting boundaries is essential for protecting your energy and living in alignment with your worth. This guide provides practical steps to identify, communicate, and maintain healthy boundaries.

- **Identify Your Limits**
  - Reflect on situations or relationships that leave you feeling drained or resentful.
  - Write down where you need to set boundaries.
- **Script for Communicating Boundaries**
  - Use this template to express your boundaries clearly and respectfully:
- *"I value our relationship, and in order to maintain it, I need to [state your boundary, e.g., 'have uninterrupted time to focus on my priorities']. I hope you can understand and respect this."*
- Boundary Maintenance Tips
  - Practice saying no without guilt.
  - Stay consistent in enforcing your boundaries.
  - Remind yourself that boundaries are acts of self-care, not selfishness.

Appendix B: Recommended Resources for Growth and Healing

Books

- *The Gifts of Imperfection by Brené Brown*
- *Radical Acceptance by Tara Brach*

- *Untamed by Glennon Doyle*

Podcasts

- *Unlocking Us* by Brené Brown
- *On Purpose* with Jay Shetty
- *Therapy for Black Girls*

Apps and Tools

- **Headspace**: For mindfulness and meditation.
- **Day One**: A journaling app to track your reflections.
- **Shine**: For daily affirmations and self-care tips.

Support Networks

- Local and online self-development groups.
- Therapy platforms like **BetterHelp** or **Talkspace**.

Appendix C: About the Author

Meet Sabrina

Sabrina is a mindset coach, speaker, and author dedicated to helping individuals reclaim their self-worth and live authentically. Drawing from her personal journey of overcoming self-doubt and redefining her identity, Sabrina uses her experience to guide others toward healing and empowerment.

Her coaching style combines empathy, intuition, and actionable strategies to create lasting transformation. Sabrina's approach has touched countless lives, inspiring clients to embrace their value and build lives that reflect their worth.

When Sabrina isn't coaching or writing, she enjoys quiet moments with her journal, deep conversations with loved ones, and creating spaces where people feel seen and supported.

A Personal Note

"I wrote this book for anyone who has ever doubted their worth. My journey hasn't been perfect, but it has been transformative, and I want you to know that the same transformation is possible for you. Wherever you are in your story, remember this: you are enough, just as you are."

– Sabrina

Book Blurb

Rediscovering Your Worth: Embracing Self-Love to Open Doors to an Amazing Life

By Sabrina

Have you ever questioned if you were enough, enough to be loved, respected, and truly fulfilled? You're not alone. In this transformative workbook, Sabrina invites you to embark on a deeply personal and practical journey to break free from self-doubt, reclaim your worth, and design a life that reflects your true value.

More than just a book, **Rediscovering Your Worth** is a hands-on guide filled with heartfelt encouragement, inspirational stories, and powerful exercises to help you turn insights into action. Inside, you'll find:

- Guided reflections to uncover and challenge limiting beliefs.

- Actionable tools for setting healthy boundaries and embracing self-love.

- Step-by-step exercises to create a vision for a life aligned with your values.

- Worksheets and templates to track your progress and make lasting changes.

- Real-life client testimonials to remind you that transformation is possible.

- Drawing from her own story of heartbreak and healing, as well as years of coaching others, Sabrina provides the support and strategies you need to create a life of confidence, resilience, and authenticity.

- Whether you're starting fresh or seeking deeper alignment with your true self, **Rediscovering Your Worth** isn't just a book, it's a roadmap, a companion, and a workbook to guide you every step of the way. Your journey to self-worth begins here. Are you ready to take the first step?.

Made in the USA
Columbia, SC
20 December 2024

50237380R00093